50

Hillside Guides - Across the North

Yorkshire River Photobooks
• JOURNEY OF THE WHARFE

Easy Walks • 50 YORKSHIRE WALKS FOR ALL

Short Scenic Walks (30 Walks)
• NORTH YORK MOORS   • HARROGATE & NIDDERDALE

Short Scenic Walks (20 Walks)
• UPPER WHARFEDALE   • INGLETON/WESTERN DALES   • RIBBLESDALE
• MALHAMDALE   • SWALEDALE   • SEDBERGH/DENTDALE
• UPPER WENSLEYDALE   • LOWER WENSLEYDALE
• ILKLEY/WASHBURN VALLEY   • AIRE VALLEY   • HAWORTH
• HEBDEN BRIDGE   • AROUND PENDLE   • RIBBLE VALLEY   • BOWLAND

Walking in Yorkshire - North/East (25 Walks)
• NORTH YORK MOORS South/West   • NORTH YORK MOORS North/East
• YORKSHIRE WOLDS   • HOWARDIAN HILLS & VALE OF YORK

Walking in Yorkshire - West/South/Mid (25 Walks)
• AIRE VALLEY & BRONTE COUNTRY   • HARROGATE & ILKLEY
• CALDERDALE & SOUTH PENNINES   • SOUTH YORKSHIRE

Walking in Yorkshire - Yorkshire Dales (25 Walks)
• East: NIDDERDALE & RIPON   • West: THREE PEAKS & HOWGILL FELLS
• South: WHARFEDALE & MALHAM   • North: WENSLEYDALE & SWALEDALE

Circular Walks - Lancashire/North West/North Pennines
• BOWLAND   • PENDLE & RIBBLE   • ARNSIDE & SILVERDALE
• LUNESDALE   • EDEN VALLEY   • ALSTON & ALLENDALE

Hillwalking - Lake District (25 Walks)
• LAKELAND FELLS - SOUTH   • LAKELAND FELLS - EAST
• LAKELAND FELLS - NORTH   • LAKELAND FELLS - WEST

Long Distance Walks
• COAST TO COAST WALK   • DALES WAY   • CUMBRIA WAY
• PENDLE WAY   • CALDERDALE WAY

*Send for a detailed current catalogue and price list
and also visit www.hillsidepublications.co.uk*

50
YORKSHIRE
WALKS FOR ALL

Paul Hannon

Hillside

HILLSIDE Publications
2 New School Lane
Cullingworth
Bradford
West Yorkshire
BD13 5DA

First published 2019

© Paul Hannon 2019   ISBN 978-1-907626-30-2

Cover illustrations: Robin Hood's Bay; Malham Cove
Back cover: Cow & Calf Rocks, Ilkley; Page One: Brimham Rocks
Page Three: Sedbergh; Page 4: Above Hutton-le-Hole
(Paul Hannon/Yorkshire Photo Library)

The sketch maps are based on 1947 Ordnance Survey One-Inch maps

Printed in China on behalf of Latitude Press

Contents

Introduction

The County of Broad Acres is England's finest, awash with iconic landmarks both natural and man-made. And whilst many of these can be savoured with minimal walking, it's fair to say that a short walk can generate a much more rewarding appreciation of these celebrated places, as well as revealing otherwise unseen aspects and neighbouring delights. All the walks in this book fall between 2 and 3 miles in length: nothing too ambitious, hopefully, but sufficient to engender a smug sense of achievement. And certainly enough to whet the appetite for those tempted into more substantial excursions.

Yorkshire's vastness can be conveniently subdivided, with its two best-known areas being the Yorkshire Dales and North York Moors National Parks. Much of Yorkshire's illustrious coastline falls within the latter, while the two are divided by the low-lying Vale of York. The Pennine backbone continues from the Dales into the South Pennines, a fascinating area transformed by the Industrial Revolution: it includes the Aire Valley, Bronte Country, Calderdale and the Colne and Holme Valleys. This corner of Yorkshire even extends into the northernmost reaches of the Peak District National Park. Southernmost Yorkshire spreads eastwards from the Pennines to the flatlands of the Humber, north of which the rolling Yorkshire Wolds fill a huge area east of York.

Not content with its national parks, Areas of Outstanding Natural Beauty are represented by the massive Nidderdale AONB adjoining the Yorkshire Dales, and the tiny Howardian Hills AONB adjoining the North York Moors. Nidderdale's neighbours of Wensleydale, Wharfedale, Swaledale, Ribblesdale, Malhamdale and Dentdale are household names, while the North York Moors feature the escarpments of the Cleveland and Hambleton Hills, the major valley of Eskdale, and a host of parallel valleys including Ryedale, Farndale and Rosedale.

Most of Yorkshire's diverse aspects are covered here, even though some favourites have no doubt been omitted. These satisfying little strolls will lead you to castles, coastal cliffs, canals and crags; market towns, monuments, mansions and moorland. From the White Horse of Kilburn to Ilkley Moor; from Robin Hood's Bay to Ribblehead Viaduct you will discover wildlife havens and historic gems, picture-postcard villages and outstanding views. Listed opposite is a selection of specific features encountered on the walks.

Each walk forms a self-contained double-page spread, essential information being followed by a concise route description. Dovetailed in between are snippets of information on features along the way. Start point postcodes are a rough guide only for those with 'satnav': grid references are more precise! The sketch maps serve only to identify the location of the routes, and whilst the description should be sufficient to guide you around, the appropriate Ordnance Survey 1:25,000 scale Explorer map is unsurpassed. It also gives the option to vary walks as desired, giving a much improved picture of your surroundings and the availability of any linking paths for shortening or lengthening walks.

Whilst none of these strolls requires superhuman endeavours, be aware there is inevitably a certain amount of physical effort involved. Whilst some walks are virtually flat, others feature a modest amount of uphill work, and even undemanding sections of path can be slippery in poor weather: in other words, go steady!

Abbey..................... 1•9•14•18•32
Ancient/Medieval... 1•5•47•50
Art/Literature......... 7•8•43•44•48•49
Bridge..................... 1•9•11•14•20•22•24•25•26•29•36•40•42•44
Canal...................... 40•42•44•46
Castle..................... 1•19
Church.................... 1•3•5•14•19•20•22•24•25•36•40•42•43•44•48•49
Coastal...................4•13•14•15
Country House....... 7•38•42•48•49
Dry Valley............... 5•6•29
Folly...................... 7•8•47
Garden................... 37•38
Industrial Heritage..22•23•28•34•40•44•46
Lake/Pond...............2•28•36•38•41•43•48•49
Market Town.......... 3•19•20•23•24•28•34•44
Moorland.................2•16•17•26•35•39•41•42•43•45•50
Museum................... 1•10•14•15•19•20•23•25•28•31•34•37•38•43•44•48•49
Parkland..................7•36•38•48•49
Railway................... 12•26•43•46
River....................... 3•9•19•20•22•24•25•28•30•31•32•34•36•40
Rock Formation...... 7•17•27•29•33•35•41•44•50
Spa Town................. 37•41
Village.................... 2•6•7•9•10•12•13•15•16•18•20•21•23•25•27•29•30
                            31•33•34•40•42•43•44•46•47•49
Waterfall................. 12•22•23•31
Woodland.............. 9•11•16•18•19•32•40•44

7

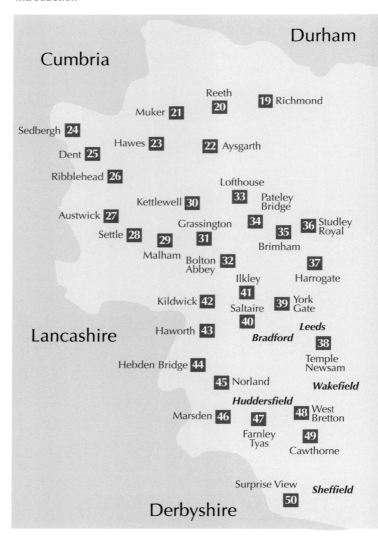

Durham

Cumbria

Reeth
20 **19** Richmond

Muker **21**

Sedbergh **24**

Hawes **23** **22** Aysgarth

Dent **25**

Ribblehead **26**

Lofthouse
33 Pateley
Bridge

Kettlewell **30**

34 **36** Studley
Royal

Austwick **27**

Grassington **35**

Settle **28** **31** Brimham

29

Malham Bolton **32** **37**
Abbey Harrogate

Ilkley
41
Kildwick **42** **39** York
Saltaire Gate

Haworth **43** **40**

Lancashire *Leeds*

Bradford **38**

Hebden Bridge **44** Temple
Newsam

45 Norland *Wakefield*

Huddersfield **48** West
Marsden **46** **47** Bretton

Farnley **49**
Tyas Cawthorne

Surprise View *Sheffield*
50
Derbyshire

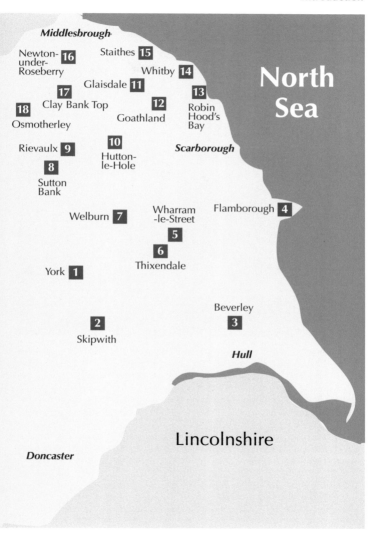

Middlesbrough

Newton-under-Roseberry **16**

Staithes **15**

Whitby **14**

Glaisdale **11**

13

Clay Bank Top **17**

Goathland **12**

Robin Hood's Bay

Osmotherley **18**

North Sea

Rievaulx **9**

Hutton-le-Hole **10**

Scarborough

8

Sutton Bank

Welburn **7**

Wharram -le-Street

Flamborough **4**

5

6

Thixendale

York **1**

Beverley

3

2

Skipwith

Hull

Lincolnshire

Doncaster

York City Walls

3 miles from York

**The classic circuit of
York's medieval city walls**

Start *York Minster
(SE 602521; YO1 7HH),
car parks nearby*
Map *OS Explorer 290, York*

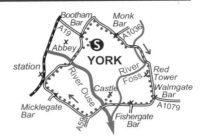

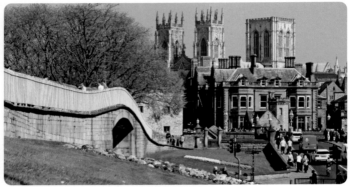

From the front of the Minster head along High Petergate, with Dean Court Hotel on your left. This quickly arrives at Bootham Bar on the City Wall. Largely 14th century with an 11th century arch, it is one of four principal gateways – all of which you visit. Ascend steps to join the Wall, passing through big gates within the bar to head away east. This first stage enjoys a long, unbroken run with the Minster on your right. From a corner with seats the Wall turns right, a narrow section passing a small turret before reaching Monk Bar, largest of the four main bars. Descend steps to cross the road and resume on the other side until steps down onto a busy crossroads at Layerthorpe Bridge. The Wall is absent here as the River Foss provided defence. Cross the road on your right, and resume on Foss Islands Road with the river on your right.

When the Foss curves away from the road keep straight on the footway, crossing Navigation Road to reach the brick Red Tower of 1490. Here the Wall recommences to soon reach Walmgate Bar, where you drop to the road: this third great bar retains a 14th century barbican. Re-ascend to reach Fishergate Bar, and dropping to a traffic-free road, re-ascend to reach a nice corner, turning sharp right and down steps to the road at Fishergate Postern Tower of 1505. With no Wall, cross a side road and on Tower Street over the Foss. Across the bridge on your right is a watermill in the Castle Museum grounds. A little further reveals Clifford's Tower, the imposing 13th century keep of York Castle.

Cross the road on your left at the pedestrian crossing and into Tower Gardens, going left with the River Ouse to Skeldergate Bridge. Cross it and a side road on your right to steeper steps at a small tower taking you back onto the Wall. A wooded mound on your right is Baille Hill, site of a timber castle built a year after the original Clifford's Tower to help guard the river approach. An open section resumes, swinging sharp right to cross Victoria Bar without using steps down. A little further is mighty Micklegate Bar: your final principal bar dates from the 12th century but is mostly 14th. Descend steps halfway to a walkway along the rear, back onto the Wall. A narrow section leads on to approach the station immediately outside the Wall, turning sharp right in front of it.

A super final section drops steadily down past the Grand Hotel, with the Minster beckoning. This bridges a road to drop down to 14th century Barker Tower at Lendal Bridge. Cross it to Lendal Tower (1300) and keep on Museum Street towards the Minster, passing Museum Gardens. Within are 13th century St Mary's Abbey; the Multangular Tower, part of a 3rd century Roman fortress added to in medieval times; the Yorkshire Museum; and the 14th century Hospitium. On your left is the crypt of 13th century St Leonard's Hospital. Turn sharp left on St Leonard's, curving round Exhibition Square back to Bootham Bar. En route you pass the de Grey Rooms and the Art Gallery. Pass through the bar and back on High Petergate to finish.

Opposite: York Minster from the City Walls   *Clifford's Tower*

2¹2 miles from Skipwith

**Stunningly beautiful and rare
heathland in the Vale of York**

*Start Village centre (SE 664385;
YO8 5SF), roadside parking
Map OS Explorer 290, York*

SKIPWITH

Skipwith Common

Skipwith is a pleasant village of spacious greens, with a pond as focal point. At the central junction with the pond to your left, advance along York Road, passing the Drovers Arms and a Primitive Methodist Chapel of 1868. The footway ends at the village edge after the village hall, but just 100 yards further take a footpath left. This heads away with a hedge on your left. At the end continue on a field edge outside a tall wall enclosing the lovely gardens of early 18th century Skipwith Hall, glimpsed through large gates. On again, a little path continues to a corner ahead, where it turns left to run an enclosed course out through a kissing-gate and onto Main Street. Alongside is St Helen's church, dating back to Norman times with Saxon elements in the tower. A 'Church Boundry' stone stands at the base of the churchyard wall.

Go very briefly left to a stile by a gate on the right. Head away with a fence to a facing stile in a kink, then resume with a hedge on your left. Remain like this to bridge a drain at the end, where the path swings right to continue with the hedge now on your right. Through a gap at the end a smaller drain is crossed and the path runs left the short way to the corner, where a kissing-gate puts you into a wooded corner of Skipwith Common. Take the path running right inside the boundary, a super walk to join a broad track at a corner of the common.

Skipwith Common is the largest area of lowland heath in Northern England, with some 500 acres designated a National Nature Reserve. It offers wildlife a rare mix of habitat including heather, wetland, dry heath, woodland, scrub and ponds. Over 70 species of bird breed here, while Fallow and Roe deer, grass snakes, adders and lizards also make use of the common's riches. Management of the heath includes the grazing of Exmoor ponies, Longhorn cattle and Hebridean sheep: it is requested that dogs be kept on leads. During World War Two the common was transformed into RAF Riccall, an airfield used for pilot training, and occupied at its peak by 1000 men.

Turn left to rapidly reach a fork. With the track going left, take the more inviting broad path bearing right. This runs a magnificent course across the more open heath, a delightful sandy path that runs through a gorse avenue and all the way to Sandy Lane car park on the edge of Blackwood Road. Without joining the road, take a path into trees left of the car park. Through a kissing-gate it runs on between heath and road, past a viewing tower and on through a bridle-gate. A brief open section precedes a return into trees. At the reserve boundary just ahead it bears left to stay within the trees, with farmland on the right. The path runs grandly on, losing the farmland and straight on through trees to meet the surfaced Common Road. Turn right, leaving the reserve at a cattle-grid back out into the village.

Spring and autumn on Skipwith Common

13

Beverley Pastures

2³⁄4 miles from Beverley

Dead-flat walking by the River Hull on the edge of Beverley

Start Dead-end old road off A1035 at Hull Bridge north of Beverley (TA 054416; HU17 9RY), roadside parking
Map OS Explorer 293, Kingston-upon-Hull & Beverley

Beverley is the county town of the East Riding, and a splendid place to explore. Pride of place goes to Beverley Minster, though St Mary's (with its crypt and ceiling) and St Nicholas's church also merit a visit. The Minster is an architectural masterpiece, especially when viewed in glowing dawn or dusk light: its powerful interior oozes atmosphere and has a tomb claimed to contain the bones of St John of Beverley, who founded the town around 700AD. The arched gate of the North Bar dates from 1409, while a Dominican friary serves as a youth hostel. 700 years ago Beverley was a hugely important trading town based largely on the production of wool. Beverley's racecourse stands amid the open common of Westwood, while the two large tracts of Beverley Pastures provide further common land between the town and the River Hull. This colourful old market town has several busy shopping streets, and is also known for its festivals, of which food and music feature strongly.

On the edge of Beverley, Hull Bridge provides a pedestrian crossing of the River Hull to Tickton and the Crown & Anchor pub on the far bank after the A1035 by-pass was built just upstream. Assorted stones provide a timeline of the old bridge's history, while a plaque recalls the collision of two Halifax bombers in August 1943, with 14 lives lost. Head away in the Beverley direction from the bridge along the old road, crossing the substantial Beverley & Barmston Drain. This was built in 1810 to help avoid flooding from the river. Follow this to the very end where your footway merges with the main road, and at this point take an enclosed path running left between gardens into the northern half of Beverley Pastures known as Swine Moor. Now bear left across the grass to join the bank of the Beverley & Barmston Drain, and go right with it. Passing through modest scrub, an intermittent path passes a red-brick bridge to resume in more open surrounds all the way to a gate/stile at the end of Swine Moor.

Without leaving, immediately cross the footbridge on your left over the Beverley & Barmston Drain, then take a stile on your left back into the pasture and bear right outside an industrial site fence to an embankment on the Hull. Turn left for a super, uninterrupted stroll all the way back to Hull Bridge. This splendid embankment walk passes a string of moored boats, with spacious greenery spread to your left. At the end small gates send a continuing path along to the footbridge.

Opposite: River Hull   *Beverley Minster at dawn*

2¼ miles from Flamborough

Natural arches and a wealth of birdlife on a spectacular chalk cliff coastline

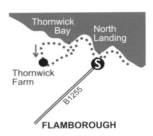

Start North Landing, a long mile north of village at end of North Marine Road (TA 239719; YO15 1BJ), car park **Map** *OS Explorer 301, Scarborough, Bridlington & Flamborough Head*

    The popular cove of North Landing features a café and WC, while down below, a few boats are moored above the stony beach. Flamborough village boasts the church of St Oswald of Northumbria & Martyr, and the chalk remains of Flamborough Castle, a fortified medieval manor house. It also has pubs, tearooms and shops. Facing the sea, take the path left between the car park and edge, at the end of which is a steep, stepped drop to a footbridge on a stream before a slant back right to regain the tops. Noting a short-cut permissive path at a bridle-gate part way, the path quickly runs around to three isolated cottages overlooking Thornwick Bay. This is a magnificent location, rightly well known yet with a curious sense of isolation: beyond the bay, Bempton Cliffs rise dramatically ahead.

    The path doubles back around and down a few steps onto a lower, firmer path. An optional detour onto the beach (tides permitting) turns right on the path. It slants down to iron steps at a concrete pill box, accessing the shore where you might opt to bear left out to the waiting natural arch at Thornwick Nab. The onward route turns left up the path to quickly level out to meet an access road at a junction. Take the road doubling back right, running along to an isolated café which makes another good viewpoint for Thornwick Bay. Here rise left onto a path by a fence, and keep left as it rises, now enclosed. As it narrows alongside a massive holiday park, continue over the brow to run to an access road on the edge of the park. Don't join it but go left along the left side of the buildings of Thornwick Farm to a corner at the end.

Here take a firm, fenced path straight ahead, dropping down onto the access road you left not long ago. Return to the three cottages, and either retrace steps to the start, possibly using the bridle-gate onto the little short-cut path through the field, initially. Back at the start an enticing and logical option is to take the eastward path between the edge and the cafe, curving easily around to further excellent vantage points above North Landing, through Yorkshire Wildlife Trust's Flamborough Cliffs reserve.

Opposite: Thornwick Bay   *North Landing*

2½ miles from Wharram le Street

Exploring a deserted medieval village hidden deep in a Wolds valley

Start Car park near Bella Farm
off B1248 south of village
(SE 867644; YO17 9TD)
Map OS Explorer 300, Howardian Hills & Malton

From the car park rejoin the road and turn right, rising to a brow with big views north over the Vale of Pickering. Through open fields it drops to a pronounced kink on the brow at the end of the wood on the right: here take an inviting cart track right. This runs past the wood end, and as it swings right with the trees, keep straight on the hedgeside ahead. A short way along a bridleway junction is reached: remain with the hedge on your left along this splendid green track, dropping only slightly towards the end to reach a gate above Deep Dale's dry valley. Turning right, an improving path runs along the well-defined rim to savour one of the finest miles on the Wolds. Dropping gently, towards the end Wharram Percy church becomes more evident ahead. Just short of it a guidepost sends the way left to slant down into the valley floor just below. A clearer path forms to drop to a kissing-gate into the confines of the site. Faced with a pond, a neat little path goes left to encircle it, over a bridge and back around to arrive at the old church.

Wharram Percy is the largest, best preserved and best known of some 3000 deserted medieval villages spread across the land, its importance originally identified by aerial photography. St Martin's church is the last surviving building from medieval times. It was rebuilt in the 12th century, enlarged, then later reduced as the population dwindled. In use until 1949, the tower collapsed in 1959. Around the church are grassy foundations of two manor houses and peasant houses. The other standing buildings are 19th century cottages on the site of an 18th century farm: on the side is the nearby former station nameplate.

Continue beyond the church to the cottages, and from a kissing-gate to their left follow a green track away to a minor knoll. From this point consider the option to inspect the deserted village up to your left, with information boards. Much of the layout is evident, with outlines of medieval houses. The village was occupied for six centuries, having been given to a branch of the Percys of Northumberland by William the Conqueror. But the newer lords of the manor, the Hiltons brought about its decline soon after 1500, evicting farming families in order to create more valuable sheep pastures.

The onward route follows the grassy cart track down to a corner where you leave the site via a gate. Drop down to cross the former Malton-Driffield railway, with the old line about to enter Burdale Tunnel to your right, burrowing for over a mile under Wharram Percy Wold. Across a wooden footbridge on a streamlet a thin path crosses to a gate, then ascends a modest hollow, narrowing to reach a gate into a field corner. It then rises in sunken fashion up the hedgeside to emerge at the top corner into the car park.

Opposite: Wharram Percy   *Deep Dale*

3 miles from Thixendale

A dry valley and an isolated village in the heart of the Yorkshire Wolds

Start *Village centre
(SE 842611; YO17 9TG),
roadside parking*
Map *OS Explorer 294, Market Weighton;
Explorer 300, Howardian Hills & Malton*

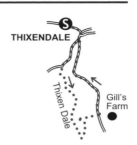

Thixendale is the archetypal Wolds village, tucked away amid labyrinthine dry valleys. A youth hostel used to serve travellers, notably walkers on the Wolds Way, until closure in 1999. The Cross Keys pub remains, with a shop opposite a thatched house and St Mary's church of 1870. With your back to the church, turn right to the east end of the village. With the pub tucked down a side road, follow the through road up to a junction on the village edge. Turn right, ignoring two early branches left and continuing along the floor of Thixen Dale between colourful banks. At a junction of valleys the road prepares to rise away: here take a cart track left through fields to a gate. It continues around the base of a colourful bank and on to a corner gate: a gentler green way continues along the dale floor, through another gate and delightfully along to a guidepost marking a cross-paths. Here double back left on an inviting green track slanting up above your outward route.

At the top is an old chalk pit and a very well-placed seat for appraising the classic Wolds scene at your feet. Resuming, the track curves right to a gate/stile, and then ascends a fieldside, becoming enclosed to emerge onto a road near Gill's Farm. Turn left to commence a peaceful return, initially between hedgerows but then opening out with excellent views over Thixen Dale as it prepares to descend Huggate Hill to a junction with the outward route. Keep right, and quickly fork left before doubling back left to re-enter the village.

Opposite: Looking over Thixen Dale   *A corner of Thixendale*

2¹⁄₂ miles from Welburn

A gentle stroll on the edge of one of England's great stately homes

Start Village centre (SE 720680; YO60 7DZ), roadside parking
Map OS Explorer 300, Howardian Hills & Malton

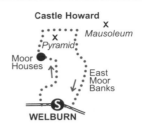

Welburn is a pleasant street village within the Howardian Hills, with the Crown & Cushion pub, a bakery/cafe and nice old cottages. St John's spired church dates from 1858, while the old reading room retains a working clock complete with chiming bell in its roof canopy next to aptly named Sundial House. Head west on the street, and after the last house on the right take a rough access road dropping away - strictly speaking the path is briefly enclosed, parallel to its left. Go straight down past large barns on the right, improving into a grassy cart track. The Pyramid on the Castle Howard estate is visible on the skyline.

Lower down, the track turns right through the hedge to cross a field. Quickly leave by a path left before reaching a hedge corner just ahead, dropping to a hedge corner then pleasantly down the fieldside to a stile into scrub at the bottom. Across a bridge pass through a kissing-gate, and up the other side a grassy path heads away to a corner gate. Advance on the hedgeside as far as a kissing-gate and go left with the hedge to Moor Houses Farm. Ahead is a semi-circular tower by the estate wall. From a kissing-gate into the yard-edge cross to one ahead, then on the enclosure to a corner one. Bear right to one at the field bottom, from where a grassy path ascends the bank to the tower. It is one of several mock fortifications from the 1720s straddling the old estate wall. Big views look back past Welburn to the Wolds. Just beyond the tower a grassy track runs to join a surfaced estate road.

Turn right along the road, Castle Howard itself quickly coming into view. This is one of the great Yorkshire estates, the resplendent house built between 1701 and 1731 for Charles Howard, 3rd Earl of Carlisle by acclaimed architect Vanbrugh. Still remembered as setting for the 1981 TV drama 'Brideshead Revisited', it is open to the public and also has beautiful gardens and grounds, along with shops and cafes. In view further ahead is the Mausoleum, an impressive circular building completed in 1741: it features a chapel and a crypt containing 63 niches for coffins, and remains the family burial site.

On your right you pass the Pyramid, a folly of 1728. Continuing, a grassy track rising from the left is passed just before taking a similar track rising right to a gate into trees at East Moor Banks. Look back for a last sighting of the great house. Ignoring an early fork left, remain on the broad path slanting down through the trees to a bridge on Moorhouse Beck, and briefly up the other side to a bridle-gate out into a field. A good path rises away through arable fields, easing to reveal Welburn just ahead. Running to a track junction, go straight ahead on the fieldside cart track to drop to the end of Water Lane. Rise up this to re-enter the village street alongside Sundial House.

Opposite: Castle Howard   *The Mausoleum*

3 miles from Sutton Bank

A classic walk along the lofty Hambleton escarpment with an array of fascinating features

Start National Park Centre
(SE 515830; YO7 2EH), car park
Map OS Explorer OL26,
North York Moors Western area

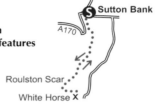

Sutton Bank is a famous Yorkshire landmark, where the hairpin bends of the A170 climb to the Hambleton escarpment: this is the only main road to tackle the Hambleton Hills, though its fearful reputation is now chiefly historical. Cross the car park on the Sutton Bank side of the visitor centre, joining a firm path that crosses the main road to an old milestone. A continuing path runs the short way to a topograph surveying the panorama westward across the Vale of Mowbray to the Yorkshire Dales. For the White Horse, simply trace the dead-level path for a good mile around the rim of the escarpment, with the Yorkshire Gliding Club appearing to your left. This regularly provides a colourful and animated scene, with the graceful movements of gliders often in evidence in the skies above - more impressive still if one should be towed into the air straight over your head. With Roulston Scar then Ivy Scar down to your right, the path ultimately swings left to arrive at the top of the White Horse.

The White Horse of Kilburn is a landmark of great Yorkshire pride. This amazing creature was the brainchild of businessman Thomas Taylor: over 300 feet long, it was carved out of the hillside by the village schoolmaster in 1857. What sets this apart from its southern cousins is the fact that its base is not of chalk, and consequently requires regular upkeep. Its very size means it is more satisfactorily appraised from the vicinity of the village than when you're actually up here! The views out, however, are far-reaching, looking south over the Howardian Hills to the more distant line of the Yorkshire Wolds. All that remains is to simply retrace steps back to Sutton Bank.

Opposite: View from Sutton Bank   *The White Horse of Kilburn*

2¹₂ miles from Rievaulx

Rambling amid woodland in a magnificent monastic setting in deepest Ryedale

Start Village centre (SE 574849; YO62 5LB), car park (refund for abbey visitors), roadside parking
Map OS Explorer OL26, North York Moors Western area

Rievaulx Abbey dates from the 12th century and vies with that other great Yorkshire house of the Cistercians, Fountains Abbey, in the beauty of its wooded environs. There is however an imposing grandeur here that is virtually unparalleled: perhaps not surprisingly, the abbey took over a century to build. It is now in the care of English Heritage. High on the hillside above (reached by continuing up the lane through the hamlet - note the thatched cottages) are the delightful Rievaulx Terraces, complete with two temples. Created in the 18th century by the Duncombe family, the National Trust now maintains this site.

From the abbey take the road north into the hamlet, and after a handful of buildings take a gate on the left ('footpath to Bow Bridge'). Cross a stable yard and a paddock before continuing away alongside a hedge. Just over it are the scant remains of a short canal that brought quarried stone to the abbey construction site. A grassy path heads away with a hedge on the right, then along a fenceside. This straight line leads to the bank of the River Rye. A sketchy path heads upstream, but with Bow Bridge visible ahead, leave the river for a bridle-gate onto an enclosed track which drops down to the shapely bridge.

Shortly after crossing the bridge, before the track starts to scale the wooded bank, take a gate on the left and head along a level path beneath a grassy bank. Through a gate/stile continue beneath a wooded bank to approach a bend of the river. Just before it, take a gate in front from where the broad path slants up through Ashberry Wood. In stages of differing gradients it reaches a brow where another way comes in from the right: Rievaulx Abbey is intermittently glimpsed through the trees during this stage. At once a gentle slant back down begins, but the path quickly levels out and curves round to the right, latterly with open fields below giving nice views over Ryedale. At a fork take the left option, recommencing a nice slant down the wood bottom to emerge into the yard at Ashberry Farm, and out to join a road.

Go left over the bridge, then left again (note the old North Riding roadsign). The farm makes a lovely picture, as does the scene by the cottage at Rievaulx Bridge, five minutes further. Across the bridge turn left along the road back to the beckoning abbey. Part way on, a short section of path offers an unofficial stroll with the Rye.

Rievaulx Abbey

**3 miles from
Hutton-le-Hole**

**Easy walking linking two
contrasting moor-edge villages**

Start *Village centre (SE 704901; YO62 6UA), National Park car park*
Map *OS Explorer OL26, North York Moors Western area*

    Hutton-le-Hole is probably the best-known inland village on the North York Moors, and in summer its popularity is all too evident. Its charms are based around its beck, bridges and ubiquitous sheep tending extensive greens. The Crown Inn and tearooms offer refreshment, note also the old cattle pound and St Chad's tiny church with Mouseman carvings. Hutton's special feature is the Ryedale Folk Museum, whose excellent presentation of life in bygone days is crowned by a first-class range of reconstructed moor dwellings. Hutton's position is also superb, sheltering under the Tabular Hills with moorland rising to the north.
    Leave the village by heading south along the street, passing the pub and museum on your left. On crossing the sidestream of Fairy Call Beck just short of the end, turn sharp left with it to a fence-gate. A path runs briefly upstream through trees, but leave it on a slight knoll by swinging right, passing through one fence-gap and rising to another. Continue briefly up the grassy hollow, then swing left up onto a grassy shelf. Continue straight up a gentler hollow, shortly bearing left to a

gate into conifers. Turn briefly right up a grassy path, quickly bearing right to enter a parallel hollow, the old path from Hutton to Spaunton.

Resume along this delightful way, soon bearing right and rising past a ruin out into a field. The grassy track turns sharp left along the edge, quickly turning right to commence a long, hedgeside stride along the crest. Dropping gently to a junction at the end, go left to some barns. Remain on the enclosed cart track which runs right to Grange Farm. Entering its yard, go left down onto a road on the edge of Spaunton. For a look at the unassuming village go right the few strides to a grassy area at the near end of the village street, noting a restored 18th century pinfold where stray farm animals were held.

The onward route is left, dropping through open country to a junction with an old North Riding guidepost amid open greens and cottages set back. Turn left on the verge, rising slightly then running on for half a mile, with grassy verges. Just as the road drops towards a streamlet, bear left on an inviting path with a fence above a bracken bank. At the end is a gate into woodland, and the path drops to a foot-bridge out of the wood. Emerging into a field, this final stage leads along the edge of a string of fields. The village soon appears ahead, and at the end a small gate puts you into a small area with seats, across which a snicket winds around to emerge onto the village street.

Hutton-le-Hole

2¼ miles from Glaisdale

A famous old bridge and packhorse trod in the heart of the Esk Valley

Start Beggar's Bridge parking area at eastern end of village by railway station (NZ 784054; YO21 2PN)
Map OS Explorer OL27, North York Moors Eastern area

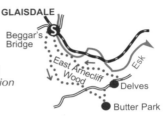

Dating from the early 1600s, the gracefully arched packhorse bridge of Beggars Bridge sits beneath a long, low railway viaduct and alongside a road bridge. Just past Glaisdale's railway station/WC is the Arncliffe Arms. From the old bridge, pass under the viaduct and take a footbridge alongside a setted ford on Glaisdale Beck. Go right to join the road, which immediately loses its surface and quickly swings left to commence a uniform climb through trees. Higher, it improves into a more gently ascending cart track. This distinct spur of Snowdon Nab gives glimpses out to both sides, with Glaisdale just to the right. With open fields on either side, leave where a path is signed left through a gap at a brief level section. An adjacent cart track heads away to enter a colourful tract of undergrowth. Distinctive hollows in the bracken are the site of iron workings which pre-date by many centuries Glaisdale's busier 19th century boom. With big views down Eskdale across to Egton, the track runs pleasantly on to emerge onto a back road.

Head off along a firm track almost opposite, running beneath a wood to meet a farm road just short of Butter Park Farm. Turn left on this to drop steadily down back onto the road you recently crossed, arriving opposite a thatched cottage at Delves. Turn right, winding steeply down with views right of the unfrequented side valley of Egton Grange. Leaving the houses it eases out a little, where take a cart track on the left through a gate into East Arnecliff Wood. Quickly becoming a firm, broad path it makes a prolonged, steady climb, passing an old quarry on the left. A slight drop past an old pond precedes a slight rise past a cluster of boulders.

On the brow you encounter the onset of a stone causeway, long used by trains of packhorses laden with goods. This splendid centuries-old pannierway is one of the best known examples of countless such trade routes that criss-cross Eskdale. This prolonged paved section makes a sustained drop all the way to the River Esk. As the causey ends, a lovely riverbank stroll precedes a brief rise above a steeper bank. This quickly leads on to a brow looking down on the start point. As the path slants down, wooden steps drop right for a short-cut back to the footbridge where you began.

Opposite: Beggar's Bridge   *Old causeway, East Arnecliff Wood*

31

2¹₂ miles from Goathland

Attractions galore include a delightful waterfall, a steam railway and a hidden hamlet

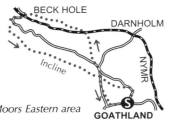

Start Village centre
(NZ 833012; YO22 5LX), car park
Map OS Explorer OL27, North York Moors Eastern area

Goathland is a breezy inland resort on a green couch amidst the moors, from St Mary's church down to the North Yorkshire Moors Railway. In between, shops, pubs, tearooms and houses stand back from an extensive green - note the stone causeways. This was the 'Aidensfield' of TV drama 'Heartbeat', and evidence still abounds: fans of 'Harry Potter' should also recognise the station. From the T-junction follow Beck Hole Road past the car park and along a short way to a gate on the left putting you onto a broad path on a former railway. This is the course of a horse-drawn tramway as it begins its steep descent to Beck Hole: its deficiencies resulted in the opening of the present line in 1865 - the replacement track improved the gradient by starting its climb sooner.

Advance along, soon dropping to reach a road. Leaving the old line, for now, turn right the short way to a crossroads amid open greens, and go left on Beck Hole Road with a splendid stone causey for company. Within two minutes leave by a bridle-gate on the right immediately before a lone house. A hedgerowed path runs on to emerge into a field. Descend the fieldside to a stile making a super vantage point for the railway as it crosses Eller Beck immediately below, with steep bracken slopes opposite. A stepped path drops to the beck, then crosses it by a footbridge beneath an arch of the rail viaduct, a lovely spot. Up the other side, the path bears left through the dense bracken, contouring above the beck to rise slightly to a seat at a corner. Just prior to this is a good vantage point for Water Ark Foss immediately below, just before the railway bridges the beck again. Though a path drops down for a closer look, caution is needed as it can get slippery.

The onward path bears right of the seat for a level stroll along the moor bottom, past a cottage and along a grassy cart track out to Hill Farm. Bear left down the access road to meet a road. Turn left over the rail bridge and steeply down into Beck Hole, passing the little quoits pitch. This sleepy hamlet boasts an enchanting setting: the Birch Hall Inn is a gem, and doubles as a small shop! Leave by a gate on the right alongside the last cottage before the bridge, and an enclosed path runs the short way downstream to the old railway, site of Beck Hole's station on the abandoned line.

Go left over a footbridge on Eller Beck, quickly merging into an access road running the short way to Incline Cottage at the foot of the incline. A steady haul through wooded surrounds absorbs an access road just before reaching the road you used earlier. Although you could simply cross to finish as you began, for variety turn right on the road rising back into the village, again with a stone causey traversing the spacious green. At the junction go left back to the car park.

Opposite: Goathland   *Water Ark Foss*

2¼ miles from Robin Hood's Bay

An old railway leads around to the most celebrated village on the Yorkshire coast

Start Station car park
(NZ 950054; YO22 4RA)
Map OS Explorer OL27, North York Moors Eastern area

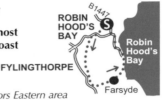

Robin Hood's Bay, with the advantages of an exciting name and even better location, will be found on many lists of favourite places. Once the preserve of fishermen and smugglers, it is now very much part of the tourist itinerary. Known locally as Bay Town, it consists of a chaotic tumble of red-roofed buildings squeezed into a narrow gap between cliffs. From modern housing on the clifftop, the steep main street plunges down to the very shore, lined on each side by irregularly grouped buildings with absorbing narrow passageways linking near-hidden doorsteps. Pubs, cafes and shops are all found here. The village has suffered badly from storms, and the Bay Hotel had a ship driven into it by savage weather. Some 200 houses have been lost to the sea, though a modern sea wall ensures a little more security. Also at the foot of the street is the National Trust's Old Coastguard visitor centre. Since the early 1970s the village has been the terminus of Wainwright's celebrated Coast to Coast Walk, concluding a journey of almost 200 miles that begins at St Bees on the Irish Sea coast of Cumbria.

From the car park entrance head away to the far end, past the old station itself and on a path paralleling the access road at the far end. You emerge onto Thorpe Lane just past St Stephen's tall-towered church. Cross and advance briefly on the road, then bear left to join the old railway, known as the Cinder Track. Initially an access road with views over to Ravenscar, it soon narrows to run pleasantly beneath the small village of Fylingthorpe. If wishing to see the village simply remain on the road to the Fylingdales Inn, past which turn left down Middlewood Lane and remain on this through a setted ford and past the last houses to meet the old line.

On the direct route, the line crosses a track at busy Middlewood Farm with its caravan site to meet Middlewood Lane. Here leave the old line and go left a few strides to turn left along Mark Lane, which quickly ends at Farsyde Stud. A continuing enclosed path runs briefly left of the buildings to emerge into the far end of the yard. Cross to the corner ahead where a bridle-gate sends an inviting enclosed path away, later dropping down to a fieldside to join the Cleveland Way. Turn left, emerging above grassy seaward slopes to be rewarded with a magnificent view of both the village and the bay. The flagged path runs on to quickly make a stepped descent. Keeping right at a fork it drops onto the Quarterdeck, then left up and over further steps to emerge onto the very foot of the village street at the Bay Hotel adjoining the foreshore. You may wish to linger on the beach here before turning left up the street to finish – possibly via some intriguing alleyways.

Robin Hood's Bay

3 miles from Whitby

A spectacular clifftop mile above Whitby's myriad attractions

Start Tourist Information Centre on harbourside (NZ 898108; YO21 1YN), car park by railway station
Map OS Explorer OL27, North York Moors Eastern area

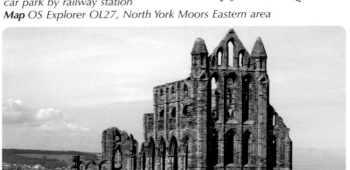

Whitby is a splendid coastal town on the estuary of the River Esk, in an isolated position at the edge of the moors. The West Cliff boasts a whalebone arch from whaling days when Arctic-bound whalers set off from here, while a statue of Captain James Cook gazes over the harbour mouth from where he began his epic adventures. Across the river, houses and shops huddle under the East Cliff. Still sold here is jet, a locally mined ornamental stone popularised by Queen Victoria: in the 19th century Whitby buzzed with workshops. A swing bridge links Whitby's two halves and its two harbours, centred on the west bank of the Esk. On this side of the river are the main shopping area and Pannett Park art gallery and museum. Here too are the termini of the Esk Valley line and the North Yorkshire Moors Railway. Popular annual events include a regatta and folk music and Goth celebrations, the latter rooted in Bram Stoker's choice of the town as landing point for his 'Dracula' creation in 1897.

From the TIC head north on the harbourside and along to cross the swing bridge, just beyond which cut a small corner on the right along Grape Lane. At the end turn right on Church Street, with the inner harbour soon alongside: note the Merchant Seamen's Hospital Houses opposite. Reaching a marine engineers' yard, cross to the slender alleyway of Salt Pans Well Steps opposite. A steep ascent of stone steps between cottages emerges at the top onto a suburban street. Go right past the old workhouse to meet Green Lane, and cross straight over along a tiny drive. An enclosed path continues, overlooking fields before joining an access road. This leads to a farm and houses at New Gardens. Through a kissing-gate at the end a fieldside path runs on with a tall wall, and continues with a hedgerow onto Hawsker Lane.

Go left for 200 yards on a broad verge to a caravan site drive on the right. From the stile/gate at this junction double back right on a broad path across an arable field centre, meeting a hedge at the end to run a nicer course along two fieldsides onto another access road. Go left on this to the start of a clifftop caravan site, where you meet the coast path overlooking Saltwick Bay. The alum-quarried promontory of Saltwick Nab on the left was the scene of a 1914 shipwreck drama when the hospital ship Rohilla ran aground with many lives lost. Note also the sea stack of Black Nab, popular with seabirds such as cormorants.

Turn left through the park (with cafe and shop) to soon regain the cliffs with the abbey ahead. A magnificent stride ensues along the clifftops, happily fenced to afford protection from the steep plunge to the shore. The path winds around to pass right of some cottages and down grassy Abbey Plain, with the imposing Benedictine abbey ruins dating from around 1078 to your left and St Mary's church dating from the 12th century ahead. Pass left of the church to arrive at the top of the famous 199 steps. Descend in style to the street below, going left along Church Street to emerge back alongside the bridge.

Opposite: Whitby Abbey   *Whitby Harbour*

2¹₂ miles from Staithes

A characterful fishing village beneath dramatic cliffs

Start *Bank Top car park at top of village (NZ 780184, TS13 5AD)*
Map *OS Explorer OL27, North York Moors Eastern area*

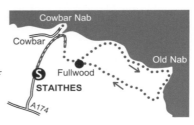

Staithes is a fishing port once of great importance, and like Robin Hood's Bay is a former smuggling centre. Descending towards the seafront its buildings cluster into little space, either perched above the deep-cut Staithes Beck or facing the small harbour. It is the sea that is linked with every aspect of local life, and Staithes has seen its share of savage storms. There are pubs, shops, a gallery and cafes. It was at Staithes that James Cook earned his first wages serving in a shop, and a story relates how a south-sea coin he took in inspired him to his life of adventure. There is a Captain Cook & Staithes Heritage Centre and an annual arts festival. The deep rift of Staithes Beck features a buttress of the Whitby, Redcar & Middlesbrough Union Railway, opened in 1883 and closed in 1958: the iron viaduct was demolished in 1960.

From the car park turn down the main street towards the sea. Keep on towards the end and depart by Church Street climbing steeply behind the Cod & Lobster pub. At the road's demise a path takes over, rising to a fork where go left to rise to Fullwood Farm. Pass left of the buildings, and at the driveway, turn sharp left to a gate. A fenced path runs along to the clifftops, giving a memorable view over the village. Caution is urged as there is no fence on the seaward side. The path turns right to run a super course set back from the cliffs. At the end you arrive above the promontory of Old Nab. This features a curious rocky tor, while Runswick Bay and Kettle Ness appear to the south.

The onward path rises steeply right with the fence, passing through a bridle-gate part way up to another at the top. Don't pass through, but take a broad grassy path slanting invitingly back down across the field centre to a bridle-gate in the bottom corner. A good path then runs along a fieldside, becoming fenced to run back to the corner of the farm and concluding as you began. For a final flourish, at a sharp left bend on the street, drop briefly right to locate a footbridge on Staithes Beck, and go right to the harbourside by the lifeboat station beneath the rugged promontory of Cowbar Nab.

Opposite: Staithes from the east   *Staithes*

2½ miles from Newton-under-Roseberry

Excellent woodland and moorland on a circuit of a famous landmark (ascent optional)

Start National Park car park on A173 south of village (NZ 570128; TS9 6QR)
Map OS Explorer OL26, North York Moors Western area

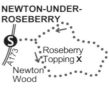

Newton is a tiny village with a spacious green and the Kings Head pub. Beyond the green, St Oswald's Church boasts a Norman arch. At the outset Roseberry Topping looms spectacularly above. From the car park take the adjacent track, Roseberry Lane, rising to a gate into Newton Wood. Of several paths heading away, two to the right rapidly merge to slant steadily up through the trees. At an early clearing fork left to begin a sustained slant up an excellent path. This reaches a path junction and bridle-gate/seat at the wood top, with a good view of the Topping. Just above you is a stone shelter, possibly an 18th century shooting box, possibly a Victorian summer house! Pass through and a broad grassy way ascends a hollow between the two landmarks to a corner kissing-gate just ahead. *From here the ambitious might opt to ascend to the top: if so, then the next paragraph is for you.*

For the summit, take the stone built path ascending steep, colourful slopes, soon curving left to rise to the summit ridge, revealing the Ordnance Survey column only at the last moment: caution is urged due to the spectacularly abrupt halt just a few paces further. Cleveland's 'Matterhorn' has a unique profile belying its modest 1050ft/320m altitude. This profile is enhanced by the dramatic western rockface below the summit, the result of a 1912 landslip. A magnificent panorama features the Pennines, Teesside, an extensive coastline, and the Cleveland Hills. Departure begins in the direction you came, but remain on the path along the crest, soon making a steep, stone built descent onto Roseberry Common. Advance on the wallside as far as a gate on the right to pick up the main route.

The main route ignores the corner kissing-gate in favour of a gate in a recess just to its right. This sends a grassy path along the fenceside base, rising slightly then angling back down to meet a broad grassy path. Turn down this to a kissing-gate just below. Through this turn left on a grassy path, merging with a track at a gate/stile and rising slightly to a gate onto Roseberry Common, where the summit option rejoins. Head directly away on a broad grassy path directly away through bracken. Ignore an early cross-paths and continue, dropping gently to soon reach a bridleway junction. Turn sharp left, a clear path heading into the bracken, dropping gently to a hollow. A few uphill steps and a level section precede a gentle slant down, curving left down to the foot of the common. The path then runs left above a boundary fence, remaining with it during several minor ups and downs before dropping via a deep groove to reach a bridle-gate. Just a minute further you arrive back beneath the gate at the head of Roseberry Lane.

Opposite: Roseberry Topping   Roseberry Topping from Newton Wood

2³⁄₄ miles from Clay Bank Top

Dramatic scenery on the rugged highlight of the Cleveland Hills

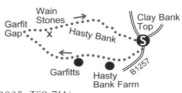

Start Forestry Commission car park at Clay Bank Top on B1257 Helmsley-Stokesley road (NZ 572035; TS9 7JA)
Map OS Explorer OL26, North York Moors Western area

      Clay Bank is the steep climb taken by the busy B1257 from the Cleveland Plain, through the pass of Clay Bank Top and down into Bilsdale. From the car park head briefly south along the road to its brow, and with caution cross to where the Cleveland Way's stepped route ascends steeply right. This is to be your return route, so for now advance just paces further to go right on Hasty Bank Farm road. Through a gate/stile follow it rising to another gate/stile, then levelling out to curve through scattered woods with increasing views down Bilsdale. Soon reaching the farm gate, instead bear right on a grassy path above the wall. This runs above the house and grounds, beneath colourful slopes and on a little further to a corner. From a stile on the left into rough pasture descend a wallside, a thin path dropping through bracken outside a plantation to a bottom corner stile. Through this the thin path bears right, through a part wooded, part felled slope, quickly crossing moist terrain on boardwalks. Across, the path bears left, curving around a bracken slope and along towards the farm at Garfitts just ahead.

Just short of the grounds, the path turns sharp right to rise to a bridle-gate. Head directly away alongside a fence on your right. As the wall below drops away, keep on to a gateway/stile in an old wall, entering Open Access land. Just above to your right the mercurial Wain Stones appear, with the long ridge of Cold Moor directly ahead. With the reedy hollow in front offering an unappealing proposition, rise right just as far as the wood corner, then use a grassy quad track slanting up to the left. This rises in the Wain Stones' direction, but soon reaches a contouring fence. It turns left with this, dropping briefly and running to a corner gate/stile in a wall ahead. The track continues away alongside a fence, still rising slightly above old spoil heaps and curving neatly around to the right to a gate/stile in a wall.

Just below is the dip of Garfit Gap, while just a few strides to your right a bridle-gate puts you onto the stone-floored Cleveland Way. Pass through and make the short ascent to the initially unseen pinnacles of the Wain Stones. Hasty Bank's pride and joy is this tumbled group of crags and boulders popular with rock climbers. The path picks an easy way between the boulders to gain the western edge of Hasty Bank's lengthy top. The stone path heads east to commence the level crossing of the plateau, clinging to its northern rim above some appreciably craggy edges: towards the end the cliffs are of a serious scale. The flat Cleveland Plain contrasts sharply with Bilsdale stretching away to the south. A steep descent begins at the end of the cliffs, dropping through a few spoil heaps to join a forestry track at a kissing-gate. Don't follow the track, instead use the stone path continuing down by the wall to emerge back onto the road at Clay Bank Top. Cross with care to finish.

Opposite: The Wain Stones   *Cold Moor from the Wain Stones*

2³⁄₄ miles from Osmotherley

A monastic gem visited from a charming village in the shadow of the Hambleton Hills

Start *Village centre (SE 456972; DL6 3AA), roadside parking*
Map *OS Explorer OL26, North York Moors West*

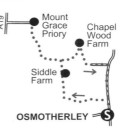

    Osmotherley has a highly attractive centre where a small green lined by stone cottages features a market cross, next to which is a stone table where John Wesley preached: just around the back is his early Methodist chapel of 1754. St Peter's church has traces of Norman work, while there are three pubs, tearooms, shop, fish-shop and youth hostel. Leave by the Swainby road, climbing north past a former chapel and lovely cottages. Part way up, turn left on the unsurfaced access road of Grant Close between houses. Soon ending at the last houses, pass through a gate then a stile and head off along the fieldside. Through a bridle-gate follow the other side of the hedge to a gate/stile onto an unsurfaced access road. Head off along its pleasant course to a sharp bend at the end, where it splits. Follow the right-hand of two parallel drives, running along to Siddle Farm. Keep straight on left of the buildings through a gate into a field, and head away with the hedge to a stile at the end. You shall resume from this point after a visit to Mount Grace Priory.

Turn left down the fieldside to a corner stile into the top of Mount Grace Wood. A path runs right along the top before an appreciable slant down to the bottom, where it resumes right. Over a footbridge/stile at the end, go right a few paces along the fieldside to a corner stile into the car park at Mount Grace Priory. Just to your right are a café and the entrance to the priory. Mount Grace Priory was founded in 1398, and forms the most extensive Carthusian remains in the country. In wooded seclusion beneath Beacon Hill, it is a National Trust property administered by English Heritage. Of special interest are the rows of cells, where the monks would have had little difficulty in maintaining their vows of silence. The adjacent Manor House also contains much of interest.

Retrace steps to the stile halfway up the field above the wood, and this time continue up the fieldside. Through a gate/stile a grass track forms, rising and swinging left to a gate beneath Chapel Wood Farm. Slant right to a gate by the barn outside the house, and turn up the access road. This doubles back right and leads unfailingly out as Rueberry Lane, with big views out over the Vale of Mowbray. After a steady rise it levels out, and an optional detour is signed left to the restored Lady Chapel, originally linked to the priory below. With views over the village to Black Hambleton, the now surfaced road gently drops past several houses and out to the Swainby road. Turn right on the footway back into the centre, passing the restored pinfold on your right.

Opposite: Mount Grace Priory   *Osmotherley*

The Swale at Richmond

2³⁄4 miles from Richmond

**Fine woodland and riverbank
on the edge of an iconic town**

Start Town centre (NZ 171008;
DL10 4QL), car parks
Map OS Explorer 304, Darlington & Richmond

The gateway to Swaledale is a remarkable town dominated by its castle high above the Swale. An enormous 12th century keep watches over the whole town including, at its feet, the Market Place. Within its sloping cobbles is Holy Trinity church, incorporating shops and the Green Howards Museum. Lined by shops and pubs the Market Place is used as a bus station as well as for its original purpose on Saturdays: a market cross is still in evidence. Outside of the square from which narrow ways radiate are St Mary's church, Grey Friars Tower and the Georgian Theatre: dating from 1788 it has been restored to serve its original function. The military presence around the town is due to the proximity of Catterick Camp.

From the south-west corner of Market Place descend New Road, quickly forking left on a cobbled way that drops beneath an arch onto Bridge Street. Go left past The Green to cross the Swale on Green Bridge, looking back at a classic castle view. Immediately across take a broad path upstream: over the river is Culloden Tower. At an early fork keep left, a broad path slanting gently up through Billy Bank

Wood, beneath a big quarried face. It runs along to a bend looking down on a bend of the river. Here a stepped option drops directly to the riverbank to resume upstream, but it's easier to resume through the trees before slanting more gently down to a kissing-gate into the river-side pasture. Cross to a path by the river and go left on a broad green way to reach (but not cross) a footbridge to Round Howe car park.

At the information panel here you leave the river on the path slanting left for a steep little pull through Hudswell Woods, passing through a bridle-gate and winding uphill through increasingly open surrounds. At the very top of the wood, ignore the continuing path along to the right, and instead take a gate just a few yards above you into open pasture. Rise very slightly to the brow just ahead, and take a stile on the left. This sends a thin path on the wood top to shortly escape at another stile. Go left again, outside the wood through several hedgerows before a very short-lived section revisits the wood via small gates. On emerging curve round the wood edge a little further, but before the corner bear right to a stile in a hedge. Across to your right throughout this stage are expansive open views.

Maintain this slant to another stile, then cross between equine enclosures before slanting right through two more stiles. Now bear right across a larger pasture to a dip where the wood comes in. A path forms to run to a stile back into the trees: ignore it and keep on the grass path above the wood to a kissing-gate at a corner where a firm path enters the trees. The river re-appears beneath the very steep drop, and the path runs along the top before slanting down a part sunken way to emerge onto the road, retracing steps left back over the bridge.

Opposite: Richmond and the Swale   *River Swale*

2¹₂ miles from Reeth

**Riverbank and fieldpaths linking
neighbouring villages on the Swale**

Start Village centre (SE 038992;
DL11 6SZ), roadside parking
Map OS Explorer OL30, Yorkshire Dales North/Central

    Reeth is the hub of Swaledale, boasting a magnificent setting on the slopes of Calver Hill, well above the Swale and Arkle Beck. A large, sloping green sees buildings stood back on all sides, including hoary inns, shops, tearooms and Post office: there is also a bakery and craft centre. Indelibly linked with lead mining days, Reeth has an absorbing folk museum, while annual festivals and agricultural shows add cultural attractions. From the green pass along the front of the Kings Arms and the Black Bull to a contrastingly tiny green at Anvil Square. Across it, set back to the right, a 'to the river' sign sends a path off between walls. It emerges onto a narrow road: go left to join a suburban street. Turn left to a T-junction, then right along a narrow lane past the surgery to its rougher continuation, with a stone-flagged pathway alongside. At the end turn left down an enclosed footway to emerge at a gate overlooking the Swale. Dropping to the river, the path bears right past new tree plantings to a suspension footbridge on the Swale. This was built in 2002 after its predecessor fell victim to floods two years earlier.

Across, turn downstream on a grassy bank which soon follows the adjacent fence away from the river. Across the river are fine examples of strip lynchets (ancient cultivation terraces) beneath the school. Alongside a gate across a plank bridge you join a firm bridleway. Turn left on this, along a couple of field edges and on to a corner gate where it becomes enclosed. After a slight rise this splendid enclosed way runs on for some time before being rejoined by the Swale. Just a short way further the path resumes its enclosed course by bearing right to a gate onto a back road. Go left towards Grinton for a few minutes, and after the church tower appears, a gap on the left sends a path down a few steps to the riverbank. A short riverside stroll passes the churchyard, which can be accessed part way along, or simply remain on the now broad driveway past Blackburn Hall to emerge into the village centre.

Grinton is the only settlement of any size on the south bank of the Swale. At the centre are the Bridge Inn, St Andrew's church, a Literary Institute of 1903, and WCs. Until a chapel was established at Muker in 1580, Grinton parish was one of the largest in the land, extending the full length of Swaledale to the Westmorland border. Go left to cross the bridge, then turn down steps on the left to follow a firm, enclosed path across the fields towards Fremington Mill Farm. Ahead rises Calver Hill, with Harkerside Moor to the left and Fremington Edge to the right. Approaching Arkle Beck the path bears right between beck and farm to emerge at a bridle-gate onto the road. Go left on the footway the short way to Reeth Bridge on Arkle Beck, over which keep straight on to re-enter the village.

Opposite: The Swale at Reeth suspension bridge   *Reeth*

2³₄ miles from Muker

Good views from low slopes and meadow paths linking two lovely villages

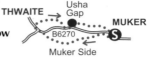

Start *Village centre (SD 910978; DL11 6QG), car park*
Map *OS Explorer 30, Yorkshire Dales North/Central*

Muker is a fine centre for Upper Swaledale, with the Farmers Arms and a shop/tearoom. This is Swaledale's most picturesque village: prominent in most views is St Mary's church, another notable building being the 1868 Literary Institute. The old school is a gallery with tablets proclaiming that the Kearton brothers of Thwaite, nature photography pioneers, were former pupils. Head west on the up-dale road out of the village for a few minutes with Straw Beck, as far as easily missed Duckingdub Bridge in the trees. Across, head briefly away with a tiny streamlet on your right. Through a gap-stile, advance a few strides then cross it to a gap-stile in the wall behind. Turn left up the enclosed green way, briefly rising to open out beneath a circular walled enclosure. Turn right with the wall below into a small sloping pasture with a barn at the end. Slanting left, cross a streamlet springing from beneath a low crag just above to a stile in the top corner. Head away along a wall-side, soon becoming enclosed again to emerge at a gate by a barn. Cross to a sidestream with delightful little cataracts ahead: in spate you might need to turn upstream to cross.

Across, a sunken track slants up the steep slope, crossing to the far wall to rise left with it to a gate in a recess. Pause to survey the splendid view, with Usha Gap below, beneath the dome of Kisdon, and Muker just down-dale. A walled green way heads away to a sharp bend alongside a tiny barn. Here leave by a gate in front, crossing a field-bottom to become briefly enclosed before a continuing track runs above Appletree Thwaite. Thwaite's delectable huddle appears ahead beneath the broad shoulders of Great Shunner Fell. Merging with its drive at a gate at the end, follow it down through a further gate then down a larger field to find a stile just to the right in the bottom corner. This gives a short-cut over a footbridge on Cliff Beck in a little ravine. The track is rejoined just beyond to run out onto the road, turning left for Thwaite just beyond the Hawes junction. This tiny village was birthplace to the aforementioned Richard and Cherry Kearton.

Turn right in front of Kearton Country Hotel & tearoom, and at the end a Pennine Way sign points the way through a stile by a house just right of a farmyard. A briefly enclosed path ends at a gate, then on a wallside through gap-stiles into a field. As the Way strikes left, you continue with Thwaite Beck to a stile ahead. Here leave the beck to cross three further fields to a stone-arched footbridge on Skeb Skeugh coming in from the left. Across, take a stile and head away with a wall to a corner stile. Advance past a barn to a stile from where the path runs between wall and beck to join the road at Usha Gap Bridge. Go briefly left to the farm and up to the house. Go right through the yard to a gate into a camping field, then bear left to a small gate near the far end of the field. A string of stiles now lead the path across the field bottoms to Muker. The latter stages are flagged: on entering the village, a little path on the right drops down to emerge at the pub.

Opposite: Swaledale meadows at Thwaite   *Muker*

2³⁄₄ miles from Aysgarth

Wensleydale's best known waterfalls take centre stage

Start *Aysgarth Falls, east of village (SE 011887; DL8 3TH), National Park car park*
Map *OS Explorer OL30, Yorkshire Dales North/Central*

     Aysgarth's arrangement of Upper, Middle and Lower Falls are spread along a short mile's length of the river, all very similar in nature as the Ure tumbles over the Yoredale series of limestone rocks to form a water wonderland. From the far end of the car park a path runs down to Yore Bridge, viewpoint for the Upper Falls (High Force on maps) alongside Yore Mill, currently a cafe next to Yore Bridge. Between mill and cottages, a path climbs to St Andrew's churchyard. Set in spacious ground the enormous church was restored in the 19th century, and only the tower base remains from medieval times. Finest feature is inside, in the shape of two superb 15th and 16th century screens.

     From the church door follow the driveway directly away up the churchyard and out onto the A684, noting the Aysgarth Falls Hotel a minute to the right. Cross to a stile opposite, and head away past a house to a stile ahead. Drop steeply to a stile in a hollow and up the other side to another. Head away with a wall, and as this bears left, bear right on a thin path to a small corner gate where a wall and fence meet. Head away, dropping to a corner stile right of a gate, above a barn. Go right a short way to another, then bear right down the large sloping field to a corner stile onto a narrow lane. Go right the few yards to Eshington Bridge. Without crossing turn left onto a path downstream with Bishopdale Beck, soon passing an array of wooden lodges at Westholme. On leaving you pass an attractive confluence with Walden Beck, with Bolton Castle seen ahead. After a length of open pasture you reach a stile onto the A684. Go right a short way to approach Hestholme Bridge, but without crossing turn left at Hestholme's drive.

From a small gate on the left cross to the far corner to gain a wooded bank above the wide-flowing Ure. Turn upstream on a good path, soon meeting the riverbank at a long, low waterfall. At a stile beyond it the path is deflected up above a craggy, wooded bank, to run on higher above. Through a small gate there are splendid views of Aysgarth's Lower Falls (Lower Force) below. The path remains high alongside a fence above the falls, and through a further small gate, is deflected higher above a steeper bank. With the Middle Falls (Middle Force) visible ahead, you are deflected left with a fence to a wood corner: a stile sends a path through the trees, emerging with the church ahead. Cross the field to the churchyard to retrace steps to the start. To see the Middle Falls at close hand, remain on the road to a bend where a gate before the car park offers a very brief stroll downstream through Freeholders' Wood to the splendid viewing point shown below.

Opposite: Lower Falls　　　　　　　　　　　　　　　　　*Middle Falls*

2³⁄4 miles from Hawes

A simple stroll in the valley of Gayle Beck, with an impressive waterfall as its focal point

Start Market Place (SD 872898; DL8 3QX), car parks
Map OS Explorer OL2, Yorkshire Dales South/West
or Explorer OL30, Yorkshire Dales North/Central

Hawes is capital of Upper Wensleydale, a colourful little town which gains greater character when its Tuesday market helps fill the pubs, cafes and shops. Its old station on the Wensleydale branch line serves as the Dales Countryside Museum and National Park Centre. Two surviving industries are today tourist attractions, the absorbing ropemakers and the famous Wensleydale Creamery. Leave through a car park on the main street alongside WCs just past Market House. A path rises from it into a higher car park, then from a stile in the top wall bears right across a field to a gate onto the Gayle road. Turn left past the creamery to reach the bridge in the heart of the delectable village of Gayle. Stone cottages fan out along lanes from the little arched bridge, on either side of which Gayle Beck tumbles over a series of ledges. Immediately over the bridge is the attractive Old Hall with 1695 lintel, while downstream is impressively restored Gayle Mill of 1785.

Without crossing the bridge take the short, cobbled way to the right, continuing along a lane to an iron kissing-gate after the last house on the left. Climb half-right past a wall corner to a stile at a junction with the Pennine Way. Continue at the same angle to a stile above a wooded gill: you shall return to this path junction. For now take the path descending to Gayle Beck, and the way shadows its bank upstream to Aysgill Force. Initially through charming pastures, a flagged section through a landslip intervenes before the path becomes enclosed for a short stroll to Aysgill Force. This proves to be an impressive waterfall in a deep, wooded bowl, one of Wensleydale's lesser-known falls.

Above the waterfall is an immediate contrast as things open out into the upper section of the remote valley. Remain with the beck on a stone flagged section to quickly reach a footbridge. Don't cross, but go right up the low bank to a fence above. Double back right with this, an improving path running to a brow and then above a minor hollow to a wall-stile just ahead. The ensuing section enjoys massive open views over the fells surrounding Upper Wensleydale as you begin an almost dead-straight, pathless march through a string of sheep pastures linked by sturdy wall-stiles. Declining ever gently, you ultimately arrive back above the steeper bank of the beck, with your outward route ahead.

From the stile retrace steps across the field to the Pennine Way stile, and this time turn left with the wall down through two fields onto a lane. Almost immediately take another road joining it to drop down onto the edge of Gayle. Part way along, shortly after the large house of Rookhurst, the Pennine Way avoids the village centre at the second stile on the left sending a flagged route across two fields, emerging between modern housing onto the Hawes road. Go briefly left and leave the road at a barn on the right. A flagged path runs through two fields above Gayle Beck to arrive at St Margaret's church. Either branch of the fork will deposit you back onto the main street.

Opposite: Aysgill Force   *Field barns near Gayle*

2¹⁴ miles from Sedbergh

Lovely riverbanks in the shadow of the majestic Howgill Fells

Start Town centre (SD 657921; LA10 5AD), car parks
Map OS Explorer OL19, Howgill Fells & Upper Eden Valley

Sedbergh is the largest settlement in the Yorkshire Dales National Park, yet its isolation has helped it avoid commercialism. Sedbergh boasts an unparalleled position on the lower slopes of the Howgill Fells: this is the edge of the Dales, and to the west of the town runs the River Lune. Indeed in the neighbourhood of Sedbergh three lively rivers end their journeys, as the Dee, Clough and Rawthey join forces to swell the Lune. Aside from the imposing fells, Sedbergh itself is dominated by its public school founded in the early 16th century. Most other features of interest will be found on or near the lengthy main street, including St Andrew's church in an attractive wooded setting.

Go west on Main Street to the church and turn down the Dent road, quickly taking a path between the churchyard and Sedbergh School's cricket pitch. Meeting a track at the end, bear left on a path along the back of the pavilion. Cross a drive to a kissing-gate into a field, and with the school frontage to the right, head straight down to a kissing-gate onto a road.

Cross and head away on a track past sports fields. Reaching a barn take a kissing-gate on the right, and a path crosses to the far end of the field. Curving round beneath Birks House, double back left on the Dales Way path dropping to a kissing-gate by the River Rawthey. Trace the Rawthey upstream alongside a sports field to the next kissing-gate, then bear left up the side of a small wood, through a gateway to approach a ruinous folly on the brow.

Pass left of the wood corner and on to a kissing-gate into the wood. The path heads away left and quickly forks at a curious walled trench through which you pass. Emerging above the river, keep right to leave the wood by a small gate at the end. A faint path runs through a field centre to a small gate at the end onto a road at Millthrop Bridge. Cross the bridge and take a small gate on the left. A good path heads upstream, remaining close by the river through open surrounds, and passing a weir to emerge onto a road at New Bridge.

Cross and take a path from the lay-by on the left to rejoin the river, now downstream. After a small bridge you emerge past the weir on an embankment. A little further, the path drops right to a small gate and bridge back over the sidestream. The path goes briefly left with it and into a field. Bear right to another small gate, then a path rises steeply left to a path junction at the top corner outside Winder House. Bear right outside its wall to reveal the whole town ahead beneath Winder. Across the driveway descend a fenceside to a kissing-gate onto an access road, which leads straight along to re-enter town.

Opposite: Rawthey at Millthrop Bridge   Howgill Fells from Sedbergh

2¹₂ miles from Dent

A mercurial stroll along the banks of the crystal-clear River Dee

Start Village centre (SD 704870; LA10 5QL), car park
Map OS Explorer OL2, Yorkshire Dales South/West

Lovely Dentdale is one of the quieter corners of the Dales. Its river the Dee runs an enviable course from high fells, carving its way down to run more calmly through iconic sheep pastures shared by countless small farms. The valley remains enviably enshrouded in a near timeless quality, and forms a perfect cushion between the Three Peaks and the Howgill Fells. Much of the walk is overlooked by the colourful hollow of Combe Scar on the south side and the more docile Rise Hill to the north.

Dent is only a village in size, but is still known as Dent Town in recognition of a once greater importance. Today it is an unhurried backwater midway along its own valley: the only roads in and out are minor ones, a factor which has helped preserve Dent's character. Retained are some cobbled streets lined with neat cottages, cafes and a pair of pubs. St Andrew's church dates in part from the 15th century. A block of Shap granite between the Sun Inn and the George & Dragon serves as a drinking fountain, and is carved with the name of Adam Sedgwick. Born here in 1785, he spent over 50 years as Professor of

Geology at Cambridge, and did much research into the fascinating geology of his own back yard. At least one of the pubs serves ale brewed just up the road in this very dale. Also here are a Methodist church built as a Wesleyan Chapel in 1834, a Zion Chapel of 1835 that serves as a meditation centre, and a Reading Room of 1880. A heritage centre gives an excellent picture of the area in times past.

From the car park head east along the cobbled street, passing the church and keeping left at the George & Dragon to drop down to Church Bridge. Don't cross it but take a gap on the left, on the bridge itself, to descend stone steps to the River Dee. The river is now hugged tightly, and after being partially enclosed the path opens out more. Various stiles and gates are met before the river nudges you briefly onto a road, almost at once returning to the riverbank via a kissing-gate. Further such gates are encountered before the river swings off to the right. Just after this bend the path cuts a corner to a kissing-gate to the left, then on through a couple of fields to steps up onto Barth Bridge.

Cross and turn immediately right along Hall Lane, whose only signage is a warning of the risk of flooding. This gem of a traffic-free route is wrapped in delightful hedgerows, initially tightly by the river. When the river departs, things soon open out more to reveal Dent ahead, across a riverside pasture. Shortly after passing the attractive, white-walled Low Hall, an easily missed stile after a short section of wall returns you to the grassy riverbank for the final field back to steps up onto Church Bridge.

Opposite: The Dee at Barth Bridge   *The cobbled streets of Dent*

2³⁄4 miles from Ribblehead

**Easy paths in the shadow of
Whernside and an iconic rail viaduct**

*Start Road junction below pub
(SD 765792; LA6 3AS), lay-by*
Map OS Explorer OL2, Yorkshire Dales South/West

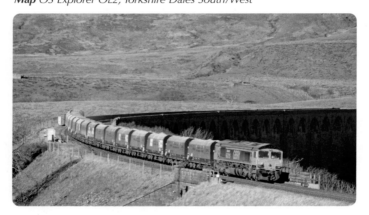

    Ribblehead stands where the road from Ribblesdale meets the Ingleton-Hawes road: only buildings are the Station Inn and railway cottages. It is the railway that earned national fame for Ribblehead, in the shape of the 24-arch Batty Moss Viaduct. This symbol of Victorian enterprise also became the symbol of a hugely successful campaign to prevent cynical closure of the line in the 1980s. All of the Three Peaks are well seen at various stages: mighty Whernside is in view throughout, as your walk is entirely upon its very base. Penyghent is behind you from the outset and will return near the end, while Ingleborough offers its most shapely side for much of the walk.

    From the road junction a hard path heads away to meet a broad track heading for the viaduct from the pub. Just before its arches the track turns to pass beneath them, giving a first glimpse of Ingleborough: instead, advance straight on a firm path parallel with the railway. After a brief pull remain on the path shadowing the line. Ignoring an early underpass, pass through a bridle-gate in a fence and

Blea Moor's isolated signal box appears ahead. Well before reaching it a second underpass is met: this time use it, passing beneath the railway and doubling back on the firm track. Ahead is Whernside, while the majestic profile of Ingleborough soon returns. The track drops down to join Winterscales Beck to quickly arrive at Winterscales.

Pass through a gate to a short enclosed way into the farming hamlet, crossing a stone-arched bridge to follow the access road out. Over a cattle-grid it emerges at a fork, where turn left. Simplest option here is to remain on this to pick up the route at Gunnerfleet Farm just ahead. For the main route, almost at once, before the gate ahead, bear right along the wallside. As it turns sharp left, bear gently left across the field centre to a gate at the far corner. Emerging into the top of a reedy pasture head diagonally away, a solitary marker post pointing to a slant down to a ladder-stile in the wall ahead. Head directly away to a wall-stile, but without using it double back left across the flat reedy pasture. A good path forms in the reeds to lead to another ladder-stile, with Penyghent rising beyond. Now simply follow the left-hand wall along the fieldside to join the access road you recently left.

Go briefly left to a gate at Gunnerfleet Farm, and turn right into it over a bridge on Winterscales Beck. Pass along the nearside of the buildings and away along a firm track, with the viaduct returning ahead. Emerging from a field the track runs on through open terrain to lead back under the viaduct to finish as you began. Directly beneath the viaduct a monument celebrates its restoration.

Opposite: On Ribblehead Viaduct   *Ribblehead and Whernside*

2³⁄₄ miles from Austwick

A visit to a geologically famous collection of erratic boulders

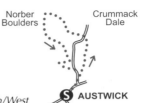

Norber Boulders   Crummack Dale

S AUSTWICK

Start Village centre (SD 767684; LA2 8BB), roadside parking
Map OS Explorer OL2, Yorkshire Dales South/West

Austwick is an attractive village set well back from the A65. A small green, the cosy Gamecock Inn, a shop, the tiny church of the Epiphany and countless cottages combine to create a scene of great charm. From the junction head north-east along the street past the pub and the school, and at the village edge turn left up Townhead Lane. Just beyond Austwick Hall on the left, an easily missed path on the right passes through a small gate and rises through a garden. A similar gate at the top puts you alongside another house, with a wall-stile just in front. Entering a field, a sunken path rises with the wall. The brow brings views to Moughton across Crummack Dale as you shadow the wall to a stile at the end onto the enclosed old way of Thwaite Lane.

From a stile opposite head away again, dropping down the field to a ladder-stile at the bottom. Across a plank bridge on Norber Sike in the shallow dip, a thin path ascends to a ladder-stile at the top onto Crummack Lane. From a stile opposite a grassy wallside path rises away to approach Nappa Scars. After the first cliff pass through a stile in the old wall, then rise left to a tall wall-stile accessing the Norber boulderfield: these fascinating rocks are scattered everywhere! The Norber Boulders are geological freaks, famous specimens of something the Ice Age brought in. A retreating glacier carried rocks from further up Crummack Dale and deposited them in their present position. What is so special is that they are darker Silurian rocks atop white limestone pedestals that have worn more rapidly away. They are termed 'erratic', and are a bit special.

While your departure point is along to the left, for now follow the little path rising steadily right into the heart of the boulders. On easing out you can explore at will before bearing left, intermittent trods possibly guiding your steps across to pick up a broader green path just short of a prominent cairn on a knoll ahead. Turn left on this to drop down to a fork beneath the cairn, here going left down to a brief grooved section dropping to a four-way guidepost on a grassy platform. Drop right on the path that rapidly curves back left at a tiny spring to follow a wall down to the bottom corner: a small gate and wall-stile take you out of the Norber scene.

Head directly away along the fieldside, part way along joining a grassy track bearing left to a gate/stile near the corner. Joining the enclosed track of Thwaite Lane, quickest option goes left a few steps to a crossroads with Townhead Lane, turning right to descend into Austwick. For a very brief extension, go right for a couple of minutes and leave by a ladder-stile on the left. A thin path doubles back left across the field, joining a wall to drop to a wall-stile in the corner. Continue down with the wall to drop to a stile in the bottom corner, back onto Crummack Lane. Turn right to retrace opening steps.

Opposite: Norber Boulders　　　　　　　　　　　　　　　　*At Austwick*

3 miles from Settle

**Simple strolling on and around the banks of the
River Ribble from a much-loved market town**

Start Town centre (SD 819636; BD24 9EJ), car parks
Map OS Explorer OL2, Yorkshire Dales South/West
or Explorer OL41, Forest of Bowland & Ribblesdale

Settle is a bustling little town that is focal point for an extensive
rural area. Tuesday markets present a lively scene when the small
square is awash with colour. Facing the square are the historic
Shambles, with shops peeping from behind archways, also a former
inn the 'Naked Man', its carved sign of 1633 being a source of humour.
Nearby is The Folly, a large 17th century house whose intricate façade
is home to the Museum of North Craven Life. Also of note are the Town
Hall (1833), Victoria Hall (1853), and Friends' Meeting House (1689).
From the Town Hall by the market place cross the main road and head
down Kirkgate, passing the Friends' Meeting House of 1689. Under the
railway bridge keep straight on, passing a supermarket on the left. At
the bend leave the road and go on a footway left of the fire station. At
the end swing right to pass around the back of the historic Kings Mill,
converted to residential use. Go left to a footbridge over the Ribble and
turn upstream on a footway to the main road bridge.

Cross the road and head straight off along an enclosed path between sports fields: ahead, Penyghent looks magnificent. At the end join the river briefly before being ushered away into a field. Cross to a prominent stile to enjoy a good section above a steep wooded river-bank: directly below is Langcliffe paper mill. Emerging again, this time bear left to a stile onto Stackhouse Lane. Turn right to reach the edge of Stackhouse, a cosy grouping of exclusive dwellings huddled beneath the hill. Just a few yards beyond Stackhouse's second access road, take a walled green path to the right to meet the River Ribble again at Locks, an attractive scene that incorporates a weir.

Across the footbridge turn right along a street between old mill-workers' cottages. At the end a snicket runs left to an old millpond. Turn right on the path running along the length of this hugely attractive large pond. At the end the path swings left between pond and mill to drop onto an access road. Go left to the junction ahead alongside a caravan park, then right along the access road leading out to the B6479 alongside Langcliffe Lodge of 1839. Cross to the footway and turn right, passing Watershed Mill retail outlet with a café. Just beyond, turn left on an enclosed footway immediately after the suburban street of Barrel Sykes on the edge of Settle. This runs between gardens then bends left to the railway embankment, running beneath it to an access road out onto the main road. Go left under the rail bridge to finish.

Opposite: The Ribble at Locks   *Heron on the Ribble at Settle*

2¹₂ miles from Malham

An exploration of the most awe-inspiring limestone feature in the Yorkshire Dales

Start National Park Centre
(SD 900626; BD23 4DA), car park
Map OS Explorer OL2,
Yorkshire Dales South/West

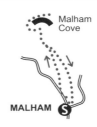

Malham has an appeal different to that of most Dales villages in that the majority of visitors come to walk, even though for most it's simply a return stroll to the Cove. The centre has much of interest, with attractive 17th and 18th century cottages. The Listers Arms dates from 1723 and bears the arms of the Lords Ribblesdale, while the Buck Inn and cafes offer further refreshment. In monastic times Bolton Priory and Fountains Abbey shared much of the land hereabouts, and reminders of their granges are found in the names of two of Malham's bridges, Monk Bridge and Prior Moon's clapper bridge. Modern, purpose-built structures are the National Park Centre and the youth hostel.

From the Centre pass through the village, keeping left at the junction by the bridge. After the buildings at Town Head the road begins to climb, but quickly leave it by a gate on the right, with the majesty of Malham Cove already in full view. The popular and very durable path leads to the very foot of the massive limestone wall rising

300 feet from the valley: imagine the waterfall that once plunged over the cliff! Issuing from the base is Malham Beck. To progress further, retrace steps a little to climb firm steps round the left side of the Cove. A gate at the top leads to an extensive limestone pavement. Fascinating to tread, care must be taken on crossing it, for the grikes in between have leg-damaging capabilities. Heading directly away from the rear of the pavement is craggy-walled Watlowes, also known as the Dry Valley.

Having enjoyed a good and cautious exploration, re-cross the pavement and return to the foot of the Cove. Use the path back to Malham as far as the first gate, beyond which cross over the beck on a clapper-type footbridge. A path slants up the slope then turns downstream high above the beck. Through a gateway alongside Bombeys Barn it runs to a small gate and on to a stile leading to a network of low walls, archaeologically valuable remains of Iron Age field boundaries. Pass through them into a few enclosed strides, then advance on a wallside to the head of an enclosed lane. This narrow way proves a grand snicket to re-enter Malham in style. Debouching onto a back lane, continue straight down past the youth hostel into the centre.

Opposite: On Malham Cove   *The approach to Malham Cove*

2 miles from Kettlewell

Archetypal Dales scenery featuring riverbank and field patterns around a favourite village

Start Village centre (SD 968723; BD23 5QX), National Park car park
Map OS Explorer OL2, Yorkshire Dales South/West or Explorer OL30, Yorkshire Dales North/Central

Kettlewell is the hub of Upper Wharfedale, a junction of roads and natural halting place. It straddles its own beck which drains the slopes of Great Whernside, lined by delectable cottages and gardens as it races through the village. In addition to the Blue Bell, Racehorses and Kings Head pubs there is a shop, tearooms and a youth hostel, while footpaths radiate to all points of the compass. Leave the village at the bridge over the Wharfe. Don't cross, but turn downstream through a small car park to a gateway accessing the riverbank. Within a few strides however, bear left to join an access road, running downstream the short way to works buildings. A path takes over at a gap-stile, beginning a lovely stroll along the fieldsides above the river. A number of stiles are encountered before a final one puts you onto the charming pathway of Lovers Lane, less romantically Hawkswick Head Lane on the map. Turn left on its narrow walled course onto the back road linking Kettlewell and Conistone.

Turn right just as far as a kink where the Dales Way is signed through a bridle-gate on the left. Just five minutes further right is Scargill House, for almost 50 years until 2008 a retreat centre whose Scandinavian style chapel is a familiar landmark. From the bridle-gate double back to a gate, then across to a gate in a kink in the next wall. Here you commence a fascinating course through about a dozen fields within half a mile. Just up above is a wooded limestone scar, while ahead is the broad, walled lane of Top Mere Road ascending the broad tongue of hillside behind unseen Kettlewell. Though not always visible on the ground your way follows a near straight wall, more than once switching sides.

Kettlewell appears ahead well before finally emerging at the head of a green snicket on the edge of the village, in front of modern housing. Turn down this splendid way to a junction, with the church-yard in front. Turn right on the enclosed track onto a back lane. To explore more of the village, turn sharp right along this quiet back lane that runs pleasantly along between cottages to the head of the village. Here keep left over a bridge on Kettlewell Beck by a former chapel, and double back left to return down the other side. Merging with the Park Rash road, continue on to a crossroads in the village. Go left here over the bridge to the Kings Head, and turn right to finish, passing the stocks just after the maypole.

Opposite: Kettlewell   *The Wharfe at Kettlewell Bridge*

The Wharfe at Grassington

3 miles from Grassington

Riverbank strolling to visit tumbling waterplay on the Wharfe

Start Village centre (SE 002639; BD23 5AD), National Park car park
Map OS Explorer OL2, Yorkshire Dales South/West

Grassington is the undisputed capital of Wharfedale, with a range of shops, pubs and cafes. The fine, cobbled square is the focal point but it is really only the shop window. Grassington boasted an 18th century theatre and a lead mining industry of which its moor still holds much evidence. Buildings of character include the Old Hall and the former Town Hall-cum-Devonshire Institute. Here also is the Upper Wharfedale Folk Museum and the headquarters of both the National Park and the fell rescue organisation. Annual events include a major cultural festival in late June, and Dickensian weekends in Advent.

From the square head up the main street past the Devonshire Arms as far as a crossroads by the Town Hall. Here turn left along Chapel Street, keeping on to the far end where it drops away left, down past a junction onto Grass Wood Lane on the village edge. Turn right fifty yards then go left along a short-lived access track to a gate into a field. A grass track bears right to a gate near the bottom corner, from where a path passes a wall corner on the right to another corner alongside an appreciable spring. Through the gate here turn right with the wall, and when it turns off, the path continues on to a bridle-gate in a fence to join a popular path alongside the River Wharfe.

Though the onwards route is left, downstream, first enjoy a few minutes' detour upstream. The path runs on through a bridle-gate into a slabby riverside area, then on through neighbouring wall-stiles to run a nice enclosed course before a ladder-stile puts you into an open area alongside Ghaistrill's Strid. Like Linton Falls still to come, this is a rare moment of turbulence for the Wharfe. This limestone ravine takes all the water when the river is low, otherwise the Wharfe rushes through and over rocky shelves alongside.

To continue, retrace steps downstream and this time remain on the bank. A sidestream from that earlier spring is bridged, and Grassington Bridge appears ahead. On approaching it the path bears left to rise to a bridle-gate onto a grassy area with seats next to the B6265. Cross straight over onto a firm path below a row of houses before regaining the same bank of the river. Two weirs are passed before arriving at the less uniform delights of Linton Falls. Here the Wharfe crashes loudly over a tangle of rock ledges and boulders, and is viewed dramatically from the footbridge just above. Housing has replaced the former mill on the opposite bank. After surveying the scene conclude the walk by turning up the narrow snicket (Sedber Lane, also known as the Snake Walk) on your bank, which returns you to the main car park.

Opposite: The Wharfe above Grassington   *Linton Falls*

2³⁄₄ miles from Bolton Abbey

**A riverside stroll in hugely popular and
magnificent surroundings, dominated
by Upper Wharfedale's finest building**

Start Village centre (SE 071539; BD23 6EX) car park
Map OS Explorer OL2, Yorkshire Dales South/West
or Explorer 297, Lower Wharfedale
& Washburn Valley

Bolton Abbey is, strictly, the name for the tiny village whose
showpiece is more correctly the Priory. Spread around the main road
are Post office/shop, tearoom, antiquarian bookshop, WC and a large
and splendid example of a tithe barn. From the car park follow the
short road out to a triangular green alongside the main road. Cross to
a gate at the 'Hole in the Wall' and a firm path drops into the priory
grounds. On your left before the church and priory is the impressive
Bolton Hall, dating from the 17th century. Follow the main path to a
footbridge with adjacent stepping-stones on the River Wharfe.

Across, the hard path bears briefly left with the river, quickly
commencing a sustained pull up the bank. Ignore a right branch and
continue towards the top, passing through a bridle-gate into denser
woodland. This now runs a splendid high-level course along or near
the top of the wooded bank, undulating along past an assortment of

children's adventure features, passing a coin-tree and absorbing a lower level path. At the end it drops down to emerge onto a narrow road as it drops to ford Pickles Beck: a footbridge sits upstream. On the other side turn downstream with the beck where a bridle-gate accesses a riverbank path for the short stroll to a broad wooden bridge crossing to the Cavendish Pavilion. Well sited at the riverbank entrance to Strid Wood, it offers refreshments, with gift shop and WC.

From the Pavilion set off left along the drive, but quickly bear left into the car park and follow an access road close by the river. When the track ends a path goes on through a gate, then with the priory just across the river, the path swings right to climb to some steps to emerge onto the road at the Cavendish memorial fountain. This commemorates Lord Frederick Cavendish, assassinated in Phoenix Park, Dublin in 1882 (Cavendish is the family name of the Dukes of Devonshire, long-time owners of the estate). Turn left to a gate into the priory grounds, and now enjoy a leisurely exploration of the priory and church before rejoining the outward path to return to the village. The imposing ruin of Bolton Priory dates from 1154 and was built by Augustinian canons who moved here from nearby Embsay. At the Dissolution the nave was spared, and remains to this day the parish church.

Opposite: Bolton Priory across the Wharfe   *Bolton Priory*

2¼ miles from Lofthouse

Old villages amid magical natural attractions in Upper Nidderdale

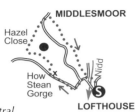

Start Village centre
(SE 101735; HG3 5SA), car park
Map OS Explorer 298, Nidderdale **or**
Explorer OL30, Yorkshire Dales North/Central

Lofthouse is a tidy village above the River Nidd, featuring the Crown Hotel and an attractive corner based around a fountain which bears absorbing words. Alongside the school and WC on the bottom road is the station house, highest on the old Nidd Valley Light Railway. From the fountain take a gap in the left corner of the square between cottages, and after a few yards of track a bridle-gate sends a path down to a footbridge on the River Nidd. Cross to emerge onto a road, straight over to a kissing-gate and past a cricket pitch onto another road. Go briefly right then fork left. Past a car park keep right as the road runs to the entrance to How Stean Gorge. If opting to explore the gorge, pay entrance fees at the cafe. This superb limestone ravine is half a mile long and up to 80 feet deep, its rocks worn into dramatic contours by the action of water: deep, dark and wet caves abound.

Resume across the bridge to the car park field and exit by a gate at the top left corner. Advance to a gate by a barn, then go left across several field-centres, using gates in walls beneath Hazel Close Farm to a path junction at a wall-stile. Don't pass through but turn up to a stile above, and ascend two fieldsides to emerge onto a road just beneath the entrance to Middlesmoor. Ascend into the village past an old Wesleyan chapel of 1899. Nidderdale's highest village shares its allegiance to the main dale with the major tributary that is the subject of this walk. Its name accurately describes this position, on a broad tongue between the two valleys. Just above, the Crown pub occupies an attractive corner.

Leave by making for the church by a cobbled street after the phonebox. St Chad's is an attractive church on an ancient foundation, containing a Saxon cross. It is perhaps better known as a viewpoint, with the churchyard as foreground to a renowned panorama down the dale to Gouthwaite Reservoir. To its right a squeezer-stile sees a short snicket down to a gate. A flight of steps drops into a field, and a path maintains a straight line to Halfway House Farm. Go straight through the yard to a gate at the bottom, and head down the right side of a field to a stile. At the bottom swing left to a stile part way along, then bear left to a corner stile into the lay-by near the start. Retrace steps over the footbridge, but consider a five-minute detour upstream for the shy charms of Nidd Falls.

Opposite: How Stean Gorge   *Middlesmoor*

2³⁄4 miles from Pateley Bridge

**A simple ramble with suitably
big views and a riverside return**

Start *Town centre
(SE 157655; HG3 5JU), car park*
Map *OS Explorer 298, Nidderdale*

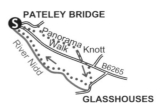

Pateley Bridge is a busy little town, undisputed capital of
Nidderdale. More a village in size, within its compact huddle are pubs,
cafes, information centre and individual shops hidden down narrow
alleys. The absorbing Nidderdale Museum recalls Pateley's abandoned
industries of lead mining, quarrying and railways. Pateley Bridge is also
home to the colourful Nidderdale Show, a hugely popular event each
September. From the bridge on the Nidd at the foot of High Street head
east up the main thoroughfare, swinging right at the top. As the road
levels out after the Methodist church, a sign points up a flight of steps
to the start of the Panorama Walk. A steep, enclosed path climbs past
an inscribed stone tablet above a well. Its poetry concludes with the
simple advice that this is 'the way to church', a reference to the roof-
less church of St Mary the Virgin a short distance off-route.

The gradient eases and the narrow surfaced way arrives at an
iron gate admitting to a viewing platform on a craggy knoll, the
Victorians' Pulpit Rock. The prospect of Guise Cliff directly across the

valley features the two surviving towers of Yorke's Folly. Continuing, the gradient eases further and levels out to reach the walk's high point at the exclusive hamlet of Knott, its houses set back from open greens. Keep straight on its surfaced access road which bears right to drop down to the main road. During this descent there are good views to Brimham Rocks breaking the skyline to the left. Two minutes along the footway to the left, cross with care to a kissing-gate just past the last house. A flagged path descends a fieldside to another kissing-gate, from where an enclosed path drops onto a rough lane on the edge of Glasshouses. Turn left on this access road to emerge onto the sloping village green: dominant feature is the tall church spire.

The village's existence owes much to the Metcalfe family, who erected housing and public buildings in the 19th century for workers in their large spinning mill. Turn right on the road along the bottom edge of the green, descending past the former station and the school to Glasshouses Bridge alongside the substantial mill of 1874. Its imposing facade with old clock and large bell is matched by a fine riverside frontage, and ongoing residential conversion includes a shop and cafe.

Without crossing the bridge take the broad carriageway upstream for an infallible, flat return to Pateley Bridge. At once the drive is sandwiched between a large millpond and a mill-cut. The river is regained at a weir marking the start of the mill-cut. Across it is the gaunt mansion of Castlestead, erected in 1862 for the mill-owning Metcalfes. The Nidd is now traced upstream on a broad pathway, with the course of the former Nidd Valley Railway regularly evident. Path and river run together to re-enter town.

*Opposite: Pateley Bridge*

Glasshouses

2 miles from Brimham

Easy walking through an amazing and colourful natural playground

Start National Trust car park (SE 208645; HG3 4DW)
Map OS Explorer 298, Nidderdale

From the car park follow the access road back out, but as it swings left for the road, take an unsurfaced access road right. Passing through a gateway it drops down through colourful country, swinging right to run a level course through splendid woodland, with scattered boulders up above. On reaching Druids Cave Farm, keep straight on a little further to just short of an old barn at a new house ahead. Here bear right on a thin but clear path through a scrubby corner, outside the barn edge and into woodland. Heeding marker posts, ignore any right branches and remain on the path which runs along the wallside at the wood edge. This remains so for some time, with diminishing trees to reach a magnificent solo boulder alongside a gateway in a wall. Throughout this stage enjoy big views left over Nidderdale.

The path resumes through more open, reedy terrain. At the far end is a stile/gate onto the access road at Brimham Rocks Farm (High North Pasture on maps). Turn right, away from the farm, and along its access road rising gently through scattered woodland. Just after the trees on the left are replaced by a field, double back right on a clear green path slanting up onto the colourful moor-edge. This runs nicely on beneath large boulders, then rises steadily above the trees and old boundary wall. After ascending a distinct groove it absorbs a path from the left to quickly reach the northerly terminus of a firmer, looping path. Turn right and remain on this to reach Brimham House. En route you pass an early viewpoint rock on the right, then myriad outcrops including the iconic Idol Rock and its massive neighbours. Just before the house you also pass the well-known Dancing Bear.

Brimham Rocks form an extensive collection of millstone grit outcrops, sculpted into wonderfully bizarre shapes by millions of years of Yorkshire weather. Scattered about the moor they form the ultimate natural playground for adventurous children and serious rock climbers. Brimham House was built in 1792 for Lord Grantley's keeper, it serves as a National Trust shop: refreshments and WCs are just beneath it. This is the heart of the estate, and the front of the house boasts a splendid panorama of the amazing boulders. The ensuing final stage gives you several options, any of which return you to the car park, with possibly numerous detours in amongst the boulders. Whilst you could follow the unsurfaced access road, preferably take the tarmac footpath heads away beneath the distinctive Eagle boulders. Quickly forking, keep to the right one to run through the heart of this fascinating area, and all too soon you will arrive back at the car park.

Opposite: Brimham Rocks   *Idol Rock*

2³⁄4 miles from Studley Royal

Elegant walking through a deer park and a delightful valley

Start National Trust car park at Studley Royal (SE 278691; HG4 3DY), accessed via Studley Roger
Map OS Explorer 298, Nidderdale **or** 299, Ripon & Boroughbridge

    The centuries-old deer park of Studley Royal is, along with adjacent Fountains Abbey and its exquisite water gardens, designated a World Heritage Site. Red, Fallow and Sika deer roam the park and you are likely to encounter at least some of them. Founded in 1132, the abbey forms the most extensive Cistercian remains in England, and its setting in the wooded valley of the River Skell is unsurpassed. The adjacent water gardens with various follies were laid out by the Aislabie family in the 18th century. While this walk only visits the deer park, it is worth making a day of it to savour the 'paying' attractions.
    From the car park make for the adjacent east entrance to the abbey and water gardens by the lake just below. Within are a shop and tearoom. Follow the drive left alongside the lake, and at the end bear right to a wooden bridge over the outflow. Here begins the walk through the Valley of Seven Bridges in tandem with the Skell. This is accompanied downstream through the encroaching walls of this steep-

sided valley, a delightful amble re-crossing the river on five further occasions by means of identical stone-arched bridges. The river sinks underground part way along. After the last one the estate is vacated at a tall gate, and a woodland path runs down to the seventh bridge.

Leave the broadening track and cross this plain structure, at once joining a broader way from the left to rise through a wooded hollow to a track junction at the top. Turn right on a broad path, soon reaching the wood edge to begin a long, imperceptible rise inside the wall enclosing the wood. Reaching the ruin of Mackershaw Lodge, leave the path for a gate in the old archway to re-enter the park. A broad grassy path heads away through Mackershaw, passing a small pond on the right and then sweeping down on a grassy cart track, with a larger pond to your left. Leaving at a tall gate, it descends a wooded bank to quickly arrive back at the lake outflow.

Re-cross and follow the track away to rejoin the access road. Go right on this to rise briefly to a crossroads with the main driveway. Turn left up towards the church, framed beyond an avenue of limes. Just before reaching it you pass the Choristers' House, while just beyond it is a tall obelisk of 1815. St Mary's church was completed in 1878 with an impressive spire visible in many local views. It opens on afternoons from Easter to September. From opposite the church gate a grassy path descends left back to the car park.

Opposite: The Lake, Studley Royal   *Red deer stag*

3 miles from Harrogate

Delightful gardens on the edge of Harrogate

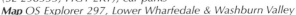

HARROGATE

Valley Gardens

Harlow Carr

B6162

Start *Pump Room in Low Harrogate (SE 298553; HG1 2RY), car parks*
Map *OS Explorer 297, Lower Wharfedale & Washburn Valley*

Harrogate is an elegant floral town with spa resort origins. Low and High Harrogate developed in early spa days three centuries ago, when people came to take the waters, either by drinking or finding medicinal value in the baths. Harrogate is home to the legendary Great Yorkshire Show, and other annual events include the International Festival, music festivals, antiques shows, and spring and autumn flower shows. Permanent features of the town include the Mercer Art Gallery, Montpellier Gardens, Harrogate Theatre and Royal Hall. The octagonal Royal Pump Room was the heart of Victorian Harrogate's spa heyday, serving celebrated sulphur water to visitors. It has been preserved as a museum, and the brave can still sample its 'distinctive' taste.

From the Pump Room cross the road into Valley Gardens and follow the streamside path to a cafe. This area is known as Bogs Field, with 36 of Harrogate's 88 mineral wells found here. The Victorians piped mineral waters to the Royal Bath Hospital and the pump rooms and baths of Low Harrogate. Across the circular garden just beyond the cafe, take the main path up the centre of the gardens: this soon reaches a wall corner on the right, just past the restored Magnesia Well Pump Room of 1858, with two well heads behind. The path resumes up the side of the gardens to ease out at a fork, with a war memorial set back to the right. Leaving tarmac, bear right on an inviting woodland path to the left of the cross. This runs pleasantly on through The Pinewoods to emerge onto Harlow Moor Road.

Directly opposite, a tarmac path rises gently back into woods, soon reaching a large grassy clearing. Pass along its right side to head back into trees. The path soon emerges to run along the edge of the wood, with open views to the right. Passing Pinewood Farm it drops onto Crag Lane opposite Harlow Carr Gardens. The North of England's premier botanic gardens opened in 1950 to gauge the suitability of plants for the northern climate, and today they make a hugely popular visitor attraction. The site was first developed as a spa in the 1840s, when a bath-house and hotel were constructed and gardens laid out. Go briefly right, passing above the former Harrogate Arms. In its secluded setting, this is the aforementioned 19th century hotel for the adjacent spa, though it has been closed since 2013.

Just beyond it at the public road-end, take an enclosed path on the right opposite kennels. This rises to a gentle brow with open views, and maintains a firm course to emerge onto Cornwall Road at a mini-roundabout. Cross and follow Harlow Moor Road's footway right to the start of The Pinewoods. Ignore the first path left and advance a little further to where a path crosses the road. Go left on this through the trees, on a good firm course to return to the war memorial cross. Retrace steps through the Valley Gardens, with variations as desired.

Opposite: Valley Gardens   *Harlow Carr Gardens*

2³⁄4 miles from Temple Newsam

Interest galore in a great estate on the outer limits of Leeds

Start Temple Newsam, signed on Colton Road off A63 at Whitkirk (SE 358321; LS15 0AE), car parks
Map OS Explorer 289, Leeds

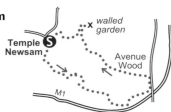

 Temple Newsam is an imposing Jacobean mansion in beautiful, well-wooded parkland designed by Capability Brown. Most of the enormous red-brick house dates from the 1630s, and was acquired by Leeds Corporation in 1922. Contents displayed within some 30 rooms includes an important art collection. From the house front head away on a firm path with the front garden on your right. At the end the broad path advances slightly left to a crossroads of ways, where cross straight over to curve down to the left, emerging from greenery with open views over the M1. At the bottom it merges with a level, solid way from the right. Go left, and a short way further, through a gate, is a junction. Double back right, dropping to cross a streamlet and swinging left to a three-way junction. Turn right, the track rising between trees and soon swinging left for a sustained climb between hedgerowed pastures. On the brow it finally levels out, and the continuation runs left to end at a gate fronting two large pastures surrounded by woodland. From a stile on the right, head along the field edge with a hedgerow on your left.

Swing around the field corner and down the far side to a corner stile, then go left on the hedgeside to a stile part way along. This sends a short enclosed path up onto an old road, the Avenue. To your right it bridges the motorway, but your way is left, improving into an enclosed green way between the audible motorway and estate woodland. At a bend it swings left and becomes surfaced to approach Bullerthorpe Lane. Don't join immediately, but merge a little further just short of the start of the Avenue on the left, revealing the mansion ahead. Parallel with the road, inside the grounds, is the linear earthwork of Grime's Dyke (or Grim's Ditch). The Avenue sets a direct course for the house. Descending through Avenue Wood it drops to bridge Avenue Ponds and rises to a brow revealing the house again. As the track drops left and fades, instead drop right to find a clear path forming, slanting right down to a hard access road. Through the gap opposite, a path climbs beneath beeches, absorbing another path to rise to the Little Temple.

Resume along the firmer path dropping through rhododendrons, ignoring any lesser branches right. Glimpsing a lake to your left as you meet a level path, go right on this to quickly reveal more of the lake. The path runs on to a junction towards the end, where drop left onto green spaces along the lakeshore. Though your onward route is over the wooden footbridge just ahead, a very short detour advances a little further before going right up steps onto an access road with WCs to your left. Through the gates in front is the Walled Garden. Back at the bridge, cross and bear left on the broad tarmac path, which swings away from the lake and rises alongside a hedge up the side of parkland, then climbing between rhododendrons to a path junction with the house just ahead. Turn right through large gates on a broad, cobbled way through the farm park, emerging at a car park at the end. From here rise left of the children's play area and up above the farm onto a spacious grassy area, and go left towards the house to finish. Just short of it you pass the Stable Yard with a visitor centre, shop and tearoom.

Opposite: Temple Newsam   *The Lake*

85

2¹₂ miles from York Gate

A much loved ridge high above the Wharfe Valley

Start *Surprise View car park, York Gate south of Otley (SE 204440; LS21 3DG)*
Map *OS Explorer 297, Lower Wharfedale & Washburn Valley*

At the end of the car park you emerge immediately onto the crest of Otley Chevin at Surprise View. First feature is the bird's-eye view of Otley: countless other landmarks will be better identified from rocks up to the left at the end. Turn right on the broad path alongside the moorland boundary wall. When it becomes flagged and veers off left, remain on the forward path past gorse and heather. The wall soon ends and the path crosses a small patch of open ground before firming up again to arrive at Miller Lane Gate. Here leave the moor and follow the stony, gently descending track of Miller Lane towards East Chevin Road. Just before the lone Danefield House at the bottom, a narrow, enclosed path runs left to drop onto the road.

Turn left for a couple of minutes' cautious downhill then turn left into East Chevin Quarry car park. Part way along, a broad path climbs away to run beneath quarried cliffs, easing out before moorland slopes are revealed below. These form a colourful foreground to Otley on the valley floor. Further, woodland is re-entered and the path meets a broad descending track. Double back briefly left up this to another junction at the foot of Beacon Hill Moor, and turn right on a broad path along the top of White House Plantation. Shadowing the thick slabs of a vaccary wall, when these abruptly end, the path and trees remain. Seventy yards beyond a broad path junction turn up a thin path just after an old wall. This rises through bilberry bushes to join a higher level path. Double back left along it past the Chevin's highest point, running on beneath a wall to quickly gain the crest of the rocks along the top of Beacon Hill Moor.

The final panorama is aided by a rangefinder on the Beacon House site. This picks out man-made creations such as Emley Moor and Holme Moss masts, York Minster, Arthington Viaduct and Kilburn White Horse. Distant natural features include Great Whernside in the Yorkshire Dales and Boulsworth Hill on the Lancashire border. Nearer, beyond Otley and across the Wharfe, are Farnley Hall, Denton and Middleton Moors and Beamsley Beacon. This is also the location of a massive wooden cross, erected annually at the start of Holy Week leading up to Easter. Just one minute further is the car park.

Winter and Spring on Otley Chevin, looking over Wharfedale

2³⁄₄ miles from Saltaire

Towpath and riverbank strolling at a revered World Heritage Site

Start Railway station (SE 139380; BD18 3LQ), roadside parking, car park
Map OS Explorer 288, Bradford & Huddersfield

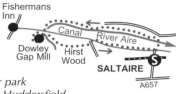

Saltaire was a mill village created by Sir Titus Salt, who moved his workers to this green-field site from Bradford's polluted air and slums. From 1850 hundreds of terraced stone dwellings were built to house the workforce of his new worsted processing mill, an outstanding piece of industrial architecture, 550ft long and 6 storeys high. The village grid-iron system remains, along with schools, almshouses, hospital and institute that followed. Most buildings function as originally intended, and Saltaire was designated a World Heritage Site in 2001.

From the railway station turn down Victoria Road, passing Salt's impressive Congregational Church (now the United Reformed Church), built in 1859 in rich Italian style, with a semicircular front and ornate circular tower. The road crosses the Leeds-Liverpool Canal to the Boathouse pub on the Aire. A footbridge gives access to Roberts Park, a tribute to Salt's work and important amenity for his workers. Turn left on the surfaced path downstream, or further right a parallel path runs past a café beneath the Salt statue.

At a corner after the cricket pavilion, take a bridle-gate in front to resume downstream on a path through a grassy sward, with modern housing over to the right. Passing a metal footbridge on the river, you quickly reach a footbridge on a sidestream. Across, go left the few strides to a riverbank rowing club. Opposite across the old weir is Hirst Mill. A footpath resumes upstream, a lovely stroll as fields are replaced by trees. This runs grandly on the bank to rise at the end onto the canal towpath at the end of an aqueduct over the Aire. For the easiest return, simply turn left on the towpath to return to Saltaire, passing attractive Hirst Wood and the popular Hirst Lock.

Turn right the very short way to cross Bridge 206 at Dowley Gap. While the towpath resumes on the other side to Dowley Gap Locks just a minute further, here you leave the canal for now. Take a rough access road in front, going left past the former Dowley Gap Mill. Narrowing into an enclosed path, this quickly forks, with the river just in front. Rise left back onto the aqueduct, and cross it to enter a corner of Hirst Wood. A broad path rises briefly through the trees to a junction on a brow. Bear left, its slightly sunken course curving briefly uphill. Soon reaching a fork keep right, and a level path runs for some time through the wood. This splendid amble passes a large beech clearing, ultimately dropping down at the end to emerge into a car park at the Leeds-Liverpool Canal. Turn left on the bridge over the canal at Hirst Lock, and turn right along the towpath to quickly return to Saltaire.

Opposite: Salts Mill, Saltaire   *Canal at Dowley Gap*

89

2¼ miles from Ilkley

Yorkshire's most famous moorland hosts a wealth of fascinating features

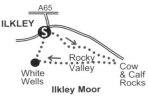

Start Darwin Gardens car park above moor-foot cattle-grid at top of Wells Road (SE 117471; LS29 9JN)
Map OS Explorer 297, Lower Wharfedale & Washburn Valley

    Ilkley is a thriving, colourful little town in the shadow of its famous moor. All Saints church has a 500-year old tower, Anglo-Saxon crosses and a 14th century knight effigy. Alongside is a small section of preserved wall of a Roman fort, and the 16th century Manor House. From the car park rejoin the road and cross the cattle-grid on your left, then immediately double back right to a gate set back. Bear left on the surfaced driveway rising away, and quickly veering away from the wall it soon arrives at The Tarn. A surfaced path runs around both sides, and at the far end a few steps send a path away across the moor. This rapidly merges into a broader one coming up from the left, and runs on and rises to drop to a footbridge on Backstone Beck.

    Across the stream take the gentler left fork rising away. At quite an early fork keep right, aiming for the right side of trees above. Rising more steeply past an inscribed pointed boulder you reach a cross-paths at the edge of the trees. Remain on the main path into the scattered plantation, slanting up and out of the edge of the trees to a fork at the start of the massive former Hangingstone Quarries on your right. Keep left below a bouldery knoll through the last few trees, and at a major fork ignore that dropping left as your path rises to emerge behind the Cow & Calf Rocks. Advance on to the crest, being aware of the drop! The Cow & Calf Rocks constitute one of Yorkshire's premier landmarks. This is a hugely popular climbing area, though the main buttress of the Cow is so uncompromising that most climbers will be found in the great bowl of the quarry round the back. Below the Cow is its offspring the Calf, whose scooped steps offer an easy angled scramble.

Bear right along the top, past the gaping climbers' quarry to a firmer path, quickly reaching a broad cross-paths at the end of the rocks. The left branch drops temptingly to a café and the Cow & Calf Hotel. Take the broad path right, heading directly away from the quarry rim with the Ilkley Crags skyline ahead and Hangingstone Quarries returning on your right. After a slight dip, a gentle rise picks up a path from the right on the rim of Backstone Beck. Bearing briefly left upstream, cross the beck and along the path heading away, rising very gently bound for Ilkley Crags. At the start of the crags head straight on into the bouldery hollow of Rocky Valley, the path running a super course beneath Ilkley Crags. At the end it merges with one descending from the crags, and winds gently down to the rear of White Wells.

This humble cottage is a monument to Ilkley's spa days. In the 19th century large hydros were built for people to take the therapeutic waters, but White Wells was built a century earlier as a bath-house for townsfolk to enjoy a dip in moorland spring water. It is now a visitor centre with refreshments, with is a deep circular pool hollowed from the rock and fed by a mineral spring. From the front a part-stepped path drops down through colourful terrain to return to the start.

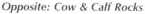 *Opposite: Cow & Calf Rocks*

 White Wells

2¾ miles from Kildwick

A delectable pocket moorland perched above the Aire Valley

Start Corner by pub and church off A629 (SE 010458; BD20 9BH), roadside parking
Map OS Explorer OL21, South Pennines

    Kildwick sits back from the bustle of the Aire Valley, with church, White Lion Inn, cottages and bridge combining to create a delightful picture: the old bridge was rebuilt by the canons of Bolton Priory in 1305, though since widened. Take the road up the left side of the church, going right past the old schoolhouse. St Andrew's is a beautiful old building, with an imposing tower and low-slung roof. Within are remains of Anglo-Saxon crosses and the de Styveton monument of 1307. Cross the arched Parson's Bridge on the Leeds-Liverpool Canal, and a flagged snicket rises to a stile into a slim pasture, rising, still flagged, to a higher one onto a driveway, with a road just above. Just to the right is the splendid 17th century manor house of Kildwick Hall.

    The route goes left, soon leaving the road opposite Starkey Lane by a briefly enclosed path on the right. Through a kissing-gate it rises onto the edge of Farnhill Moor, whose heathery surrounds quickly open out. The main path heads directly away, rising gently and running to the farm at Crag Top. Through a gate to its left the main body of the moor is underfoot. At a near immediate fork remain on the main path to the left, rising above old quarries and then more thinly but always clearly through bracken, scrub and scattered trees before rising again to the Jubilee Tower. Locally 'Farnhill Pinnacle', this 12ft monument was erected for Queen Victoria's Golden Jubilee in 1887. Across the valley is Cononley, while meandering below is a good length of the canal: down-dale Earl Crag and its monuments patrol the skyline, while behind Skipton town the peaks of Flasby Fell are prominent.

Leave by returning to the path crossroads a few yards east of the pinnacle, turning left on a clear path to maintain your earlier direction. Rising slightly through bracken and scattered silver birch into heather, it bears right to quickly meet a wall. Turn left here on a thinner but very clear wallside path, soon commencing a steady descent. Part way down, remain on the main path as it veers off left. This angles down far more gently, entering scattered silver birch and becoming largely level. After a splendid few minutes it emerges from denser trees and forks. Take the thinner but still clear path slanting down to the right, soon dropping to reach an old walled reservoir. Here a broader path slants right the short way down onto a back road above Farnhill Wood

Go left down into Farnhill, and at the junction turn right. The road winds down to a sharp right bend immediately after a splendid barn: here take an old kissing-gate in the recess on the left. A faint path remains with the wall as it swings sharp left, with Farnhill Hall in trees on your right. Dropping down to approach the canal, bear right to a stile accessing Milking Hill swing-bridge. Across, go left on the tow-path to return to the start. Near the end Farnhill's canalside buildings are on parade before crossing the street on an aqueduct to conclude.

Opposite: At Farnhill Pinnacle   *Aire Valley from Farnhill Moor*

2¹₂ miles from Haworth

**Easy moorland walking around a
world famous literary landscape**

Start Parish church (SE 029372;
BD22 8DP), car parks   *Map* OS Explorer OL21, South Pennines

Haworth ceased to be just another village in the 19th century
when the literary fame of the Bronte sisters Charlotte, Emily and Anne
spread. Lined with shops and cafes, the main street climbs steeply to
St Michael's church, surrounded by pubs. Inside, the Bronte Vault
holds the remains of all but Anne, whose grave overlooks the sea at
Scarborough. Behind the church is the Georgian parsonage of 1779,
now a museum of its former occupants. Haworth station is home to the
village's other major attraction, the Keighley & Worth Valley Railway.
This hugely popular preserved line sees steam trains chugging up and
down the valley between Keighley and Oxenhope.

From the top of the setted main street, ascend the steps and pass
right of the church onto a setted road. This rises past the churchyard
and former school to Bronte Parsonage. Just past it an enclosed path
takes over, running between fields and housing to emerge at the end
via a small gate into a field. A century and a half ago the sisters would
have taken this route to the moors where they found inspiration. The
part flagged path runs straight on to an old stile onto West Lane at the
village edge. Go left and immediately left again on Cemetery Road,

with a verge path rising onto the moorland slopes of Penistone Hill. Big views look over the Worth Valley, with Lower Laithe Reservoir ahead.

Just past a parking area opposite a cemetery, take a broad, grassy path slanting down towards Lower Laithe Reservoir: off the moor it becomes enclosed above waterworks buildings to run a surfaced course out onto a road by the dam. Stanbury sits on its little ridge across the water. Turn left on the footway uphill, quickly returning to the edge of Penistone Hill at a junction. With open moorland all around, turn very briefly right on a rough road. Before the cattle-grid, take a clear path doubling back left up the moor to rapidly meet the road again.

Cross straight over onto a continuation path slanting up towards heather colonised spoil heaps. In front of them you alight onto a firm path. Again cross straight over onto a nicer path slanting gently right up beneath the heathery mounds, soon merging into a stony access road. Big views look right to Oxenhope beneath Ovenden Moor windfarm. Rise briefly left to a large parking area on the brow of Penistone Hill. Man's workshop has become his playground, its former quarries put to use as car parks. Immediately beyond it the track forks: take the main, left one past a massive quarry hole to a cricket pavilion just ahead.

A continuing firm path squeezes between quarry and cricket pitch, then bears left across the moor between the hole and the wall. Keeping left of further old quarries it runs past an OS column just to the left to drop down to a major cross-paths at a 'Literary Landscape' sculpture. Turn right to slant gently down to quickly reach a moor-edge road, across which descend the drive to Sowdens. Remain on the enclosed track continuing beneath it to a T-junction of ways. Take the path left, which runs firmly on past allotments to return to the church.

Opposite: On Penistone Hill   *Haworth's main street*

Heptonstall

3 miles from Hebden Bridge

A steep haul to an iconic hilltop village from an iconic valley town, with dramatic views

Start Old bridge on Bridge Gate in centre (SD 991272; HX7 8EX), car parks
Map OS Explorer OL21, South Pennines

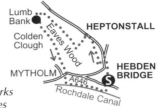

Hebden Bridge is focal point of Upper Calderdale, its houses climbing alarmingly up steep hillsides. The lively centre boasts myriad attractions, including a visitor centre on the Rochdale Canal. On Bridge Gate cross the packhorse bridge over Hebden Water and cross to The Buttress, a relentlessly steep cobbled way. With big views back over town it passes a Methodist burial ground before joining a level road at the top. Go left a few strides to an old milestone at a junction, then ascend an access road opposite. Beyond the second house it ends at a small quarry site. Just before it, a part enclosed path heads off right, rising gently through part wooded surrounds, curving around and up to emerge via the front of a short terrace onto a road at the foot of Heptonstall. Turn left up past the Post office/shop and tearoom.

Heptonstall is a fascinating hilltop village steeped in history. Focal point is where the churchyard separates the imposing church of 1854 from the part 13th century old church. Alongside is the grammar school of 1772, now a museum. Seek out also the octagonal Wesleyan chapel (1764), the old dungeon (1824) and the 16th century Cloth Hall. Leave the main street between the Cross Inn and the White Lion, by an enclosed path on the left. Passing the museum it enters the old churchyard. Advance to the new church, and a path goes left out onto a rough lane. Bear right on this, quickly crossing a suburban road. Just a little further at a fork, ignore the cart track bearing left and take the surfaced path bearing right. This runs between more gardens, over another road then escapes to emerge onto the crest of Eaves Wood.

Dramatic views from airy gritstone outcrops look over Colden Clough to Stoodley Pike, seen from valley floor to towering monument. Turn right on a splendid high-level path above the wooded clough. Keeping to the upper path, the later stages feature a gentle clamber through the bouldery wood top before joining an access road. Turn down this a short way, ignoring a level path striking off right. Just below, as a path crosses the road, double back left into trees. It drops steeply past Lumb Bank Cottage, then more gently along the base of the wood.

Levelling out, it runs a long, broad course along the foot of Eaves Wood. Soon entirely in woodland, you later pass above a line of red-brick houses and simply forge straight on through a gate. Near the end the main way drops to another gate, and runs a briefly enclosed course down onto an access road at Mytholm. Go left on this, soon diverted around the right side of the end house, above a steep wooded bank opposite the church. Resuming through trees it quickly drops down to a path junction at old gateposts, and slants down and out onto the A646. Go briefly right on the footway to cross at a pedestrian island, and after bridging Colden Water turn down steps as an urban path shadows the beck to its confluence with the Calder. A footbridge across this points straight ahead up onto the canal towpath. Turn left for a quick return, passing several locks. Leave just after bridging the river, dropping left onto Holme Street back into the centre.

Opposite: Heptonstall   *Eaves Wood*

3 miles from Norland

A colourful stroll around a popular pocket moorland above Calderdale

Start *Crossroads of Shaw Lane, Clough Road and Berry Moor Road by war memorial (SE 065224; HX6 3RN). Car park off Shaw Lane, along a short rough track by a play area on a corner of the moor.*

NORLAND

Moorcock Inn

Ladstone x Rock

Norland Moor

Clough Moor Bridge

Map *OS Explorer OL21, South Pennines*

Norland is an isolated hilltop settlement boasting splendid old clothiers' houses: St Luke's church, a school and a fine old milestone are all centrally placed. Norland Moor is an island-like heather tract perched high above Sowerby Bridge and the Ryburn Valley. It bears the much-healed scars of extensive small-scale quarrying, notably along its western escarpment. From the car park take a broad path rising diagonally away to heathery old quarries on the brow. Forking within 50 strides, keep left to rise to a crossroads with a broader path. Turn right to rise very gently across the moor, passing above old quarry sites and along a gentle but obvious edge.

Beyond a covered reservoir where the Calderdale Way departs left, the more extensive quarries of Turgate Delph are passed, totally reclaimed by heather. Just below on the roadside is the Moorcock Inn. Forging on above the quarries, the main path bears left to an Ordnance

Survey column at 931ft/284m. At the junction here turn right to regain the edge at the prominent Ladstone Rock. This gritstone outcrop is a distinctive landmark with extensive views westwards over the Ryburn Valley featuring Crow Hill, Great Manshead Hill, Rishworth Moor, Blackstone Edge and the moors south of the M62.

Resuming along the edge, the path soon drops towards the road. Without actually setting foot on tarmac, advance straight on a parallel path to the moor corner, with some chalets behind. Here take a clear path left to remain on the moor edge, rising by a wall. It soon gently veers away from it to a path junction at an outer wall corner. Now bear right on the splendid wallside path, enjoying a very gentle decline through colourful vegetation. Reaching another corner, an enclosed way runs straight on, but you go left to again remain on the moor. Initially between walls, it then drops slightly to another outer corner. At this path crossroads go right to resume as before, on a broader path again gently declining with the boundary wall just to your right. Ignore a branch left and remain on the path near the moor edge, curving round to the left to absorb the Calderdale Way at a solid cairn.

Ahead, the Wainhouse Tower can be discerned across the Calder Valley, completely dwarfing the mill chimneys and church spires. This famous landmark was built in the 1870s supposedly to serve a dye-works, and is usually open for ascents on public holidays. Keep on to a wall corner near the edge of the moor. At this major path junction under a pylon, double back left on a very broad path rising gently back across the moor. Within five minutes turn off right at right-angles on a broad, clear path running a level course, over a cross-paths and quickly revealing the car park just a couple of minutes further.

Opposite: On Norland Moor   *Ladstone Rock*

3 miles from Marsden

**Towpath and fieldpath walking
at a famous trans-Pennine tunnel**

Start Railway station
(SE 046118; HD7 6DH), car park
Map OS Explorer OL21, South Pennines

Marsden is the first settlement in the Colne Valley, large textile mills and terraced rows typifying this former manufacturing village at the heart of the Luddite movement. Outside St Bartholomew's church is the tomb of machine-maker Enoch Taylor: those who feared machines would take their jobs famously gave his name to the tools they used to smash them. Facing the station, go left to join the Huddersfield Narrow Canal at a lock, and go left on the towpath for a pleasant ten minutes. Under low railway bridges you emerge opposite a visitor centre in a restored warehouse at Tunnel End: just past it, rise to a bridge.

The canal's focal point features a café by Standedge Tunnel entrance. Boat trips range from short forays into the tunnel to full-length journeys. Opened in 1811, the canal conveyed goods between towns either side of the Pennines, and the impasse of Standedge called for the highest, deepest and longest canal tunnel in the land. Railway competition soon hit hard, though it wasn't until 1944 that the tunnel closed. Fast forward 30 years, and with just six locks remaining open, a restoration programme culminated at the start of the 21st century in the tunnel's re-opening. The parallel railway tunnels of 1848 and 1871 were sidelined by a third tunnel of 1894, now the only one in use.

Cross the bridge and head up the road to a junction with Waters Road by the former Tunnel End Inn. Climb past it, through a gate and up a path at a driveway. Pass left of the house above, up the tapering garden to a gate onto a rough access road. Turn left past several houses, and becoming surfaced, you soon reach a junction. Don't drop away, but take the right option maintaining a higher course to two more houses. It ends abruptly just before the last one where a walled footway takes over, passing to its right. Quickly emerging into open slopes beneath Great Edge it advances invitingly away, rising gently to a bridle-gate in a fence. The path drops slightly, winding round to the right and on past a low ruin. A flagged path drops to a streamlet in Park Clough, across which double back a few yards then climb by a wall to a gate at the top.

Don't join the road, but double back left down the field, slanting gently away to find a clearer path above a steep drop to reach a stile. A fenceside path drops down outside the clough, through another old stile and along an enclosed course to emerge onto Blake Lea Lane. Turn left on Waters Road beneath Hey Green House. On your left a generator from around 1890 used water power to provide electricity to light mill-owner Joseph Crowther's 'big house'. After the terrace of Lower Hey Green, take a bridle-gate on the right. A firm path runs alongside the beck and then the drained Tunnel End Reservoir. At the end drop right between houses and the embankment to a gateway onto a road. Cross over and down a grassy area to return to Tunnel End. Now simply retrace opening steps along the towpath.

Opposite: Tunnel End　　　　　　　　　　　*Huddersfield Narrow Canal*

47   Castle Hill

3 miles from Farnley Tyas

An Iron Age fort with a Victorian tower above the Holme Valley

Start *Village centre (SE 164127; HD4 6UD), roadside parking*
Map *OS Explorer 288, Bradford & Huddersfield*

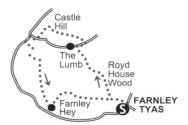

Farnley Tyas is a pleasant hilltop village. Facing the Golden Cock pub, turn right and immediately left at a junction. Within a few strides turn down an enclosed cart track after the first house. This swings sharp left to end at a bench with views to Castle Hill. Through the gate turn right down the fieldside to a gate/stile part way down: a cart track descends Royd House Wood, crossing a small stream and on to briefly emerge from trees. Almost immediately re-entering woodland, it runs a short, level course to leave the trees at the other side. Pass right of a boundary wall heading away, a path shadowing it down to a stile at the end. A path heads off through scattered trees, descending steps into Lumb Dike.

A bridge crosses the stream and the path rises to a gate. Ascend the field with a fence on your left, and up a second fieldside to a stile at The Lumb. Turn briefly right on Lumb Lane to a stile on the left for a steep fieldside climb to a stile. Resume uphill to one onto an access road. Just to your left another stile maintains the climb, becoming enclosed in greenery to slant left into undergrowth. At the rear of a hidden house a signed path doubles back right, out of undergrowth to emerge by a

102

fence with open views. Follow the path right with the fence to the end of the site, where rise to meet a firm path encircling the outer bank. Go right on this back round the other side of the fort, or at a cross-paths, ascend to follow the bank top. Either way will lead to the Victoria Tower.

Castle Hill's majestic stature is further enhanced by a tower built to commemorate Queen Victoria's Diamond Jubilee of 1897. On afternoons at holidays and weekends you can normally climb to survey the massive panorama. Castle Hill is best known for its Iron Age hillfort, its extensive ditches and ramparts later incorporated into the defences of a motte and bailey castle around 800 years ago. The castle became a hunting lodge before falling into ruin around 1320.

Leave by a hard path running a few strides from the tower to a flight of steps down onto a road. Go right to a T-junction, then left. At the second house on the left take a stile set back across its yard, and follow a wall away. At a kink in it go sharp right across the field centre to an outer corner, and through a gateway turn left to resume along the wall. Through an intervening stile this leads to a gateway in the bottom wall. Through it turn sharp right to a gate/stile above Roaf Wood, and on again through a corner stile ahead, leaving the wood edge to rise with a wall on your left. At a bend part way up pass through a stile and a clear path crosses an extensive sloping field. This runs a near level course through scant lines of old trees and on to the far end where a gap puts you onto an access road.

Go left past cottages at Farnley Hey, and at the end go right to an enclosed path dropping into a field. Slant right to a stile in a descending wall, then down the fieldside to a stile onto a path junction in front of a guidestone. Bear right on a short-lived enclosed path, and at the end cross a track to a stile. Your path then crosses another sloping pasture, meeting an outer corner to lead to the far end. At this path junction go straight ahead for a few enclosed strides into a field, and resume along several field bottoms. At the end slant gently above a line of old trees to rejoin the outward route.

Opposite: Castle Hill   **The Pennines from Castle Hill**

2³⁄₄ miles from West Bretton

Very gentle walking around an absorbing outdoor museum

Start Yorkshire Sculpture Park visitor centre (SE 294124; S75 4BX), main car park off A637
Map OS Explorer 278, Sheffield & Barnsley

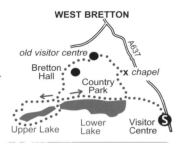

Next to Junction 38 of the M1, Bretton Country Park is a fine setting for the Yorkshire Sculpture Park, with an expansive display of outdoor exhibits. The park opens all year except Christmas Eve and Christmas Day, with free entry but appreciable parking charges. Works by local superstars Henry Moore and Barbara Hepworth feature amid an ever-changing range of sculptures. The present Bretton Hall was built in the 1730s for Sir William Wentworth: it closed in 2007 after almost 60 years as a college, and 2019 sees its rebirth as a luxury hotel, the same year as the opening of the new Visitor Centre with exhibits, restaurant and shop.

From the centre join the access road into the park, and fork left on a firm, level path running to a junction above a bridge above the dam of the Lower Lake. The bridge crosses a canal as it turns to drop through cascades, created to carry water from the River Dearne past the lakes to a blast furnace. Bear right here up a grass path, slanting left to pass through a gate on the access road alongside stone sheepfolds. Now bear right to a path in trees accessing tree-shrouded St Bartholomew's chapel of 1744. Re-emerging, the access track can be quickly left for a firm grass path slanting right, bound for the gallery at the old visitor centre, possibly by way of another Henry Moore sculpture up to the right. Pass through the building and out along the western exit into formal gardens. Drop down solid steps immediately in front to pass along the front of the Underground Gallery. Bear right on the main path to pass through a hedge gap into open parkland. Head away past sculptures to cross an access road, then drop left on the grass to the YSP Learning Building with smaller café and car park.

Continue down into the Lower Park, past more exhibits to quickly reach the 200-year old Camellia House. Continue down the grass onto a broad pathway, with the Lower Lake in view ahead. Turn right on this to quickly reach a broad access track. Just to your left is a bridge over the canal, with Cascade Bridge, crossed later in the walk, beyond. For now go straight to a gate into the Upper Lake's wooded surrounds. A broad track heads away, while the more interesting right branch path rises slightly through trees to pass the Summer House, a 19th century folly in the style of a Greek temple. The path then drops down past the Obelisk to rejoin the main way. This curves around to bridge the canal to the Boathouse and over the very head of the lake before swinging left to return down the south bank. The boathouse features six stone columns from the original building, possibly as old as the 1760s.

A footbridge crosses a small ravine, then a bird-hide sits just to the left. When the path forks, the left option visits the 18th century Shell Grotto. Rejoining, you emerge onto an access road: go left over Cascade Bridge then right through a gate to head along the shore of the Lower Lake. This makes a grand stroll past further sculptures and just beneath the canal which makes a good foreground to Bretton Hall. Part way on you merge into a stony access road alongside a boathouse, keeping straight on this lakeshore track to arrive back above the dam: cross the canal bridge to rejoin your outward route, and turn right to finish.

Opposite: Sculpture Park   *Bretton Hall*

2¼ miles from Cawthorne

Simple parkland strolling from a lovely South Yorkshire village

Start *Green by junction with A635 (SE 286079; S75 4HL), roadside parking*
Map *OS Explorer 278, Sheffield & Barnsley* ***or*** *Explorer OL1, Peak District, Dark Peak*

Cawthorne is a popular village on the edge of Cannon Hall estate. All Saints church dates from the 11th century, with a 15th century tower and Anglian font. An impressive cross in the street outside is based on a 10th century Anglian cross within the church wall. Also here are the Spencer Arms, a Post office/shop, antiques/tearoom and gallery/gift shop. Fine buildings include Lady Elizabeth Spencer-Stanhope's Girls' School, now the village hall, and a grammar school of 1639. The Victoria Jubilee Museum opens weekend afternoons from Easter to October, while a triangular green features a turnpike milestone.

From the green head towards the village centre on Church Street. A short-cut turns left on Church Lane, with a gate into the churchyard. To the right of the church the main gateway puts you onto the head of a short street. Advance briefly on but turn left on an enclosed cart track before reaching the cross. At the end drop down steps alongside the museum onto a road. Here are the village tap of 1890, and a milestone opposite Maltkiln Row. Cross and go left, curving down to pass the school. At the end of allotments, turn right on unsurfaced Dark Lane which leads to the cricket field. Pass through the kissing-gate alongside their gate on the left, and a path shadows the left hedgerow of the grounds. At the end pass through trees into a corner of Cannon Hall Park.

Advance to a firm path just ahead, and turn right on it to bridge Daking Brook amid cascades and lakes. Immediately over, leave the path and turn left through parkland on the edge of the stream, later enjoying views of Cannon Hall. At the end of the park you enter a car park at Cascades Bridge. Don't join the road, but turn right to the Pavilion café at the top of the car park, and a surfaced path rises to the 19th century deer shelter. Rising a little further to a junction, take the broad carriageway right to Cannon Hall. This 18th century mansion boasts attractive gardens as well as its parkland and restored lakes, the bulk of the estate being sold by the Spencer-Stanhopes to Barnsley Council in 1951. The hall now serves as a museum displaying stunning collections including paintings, ceramics and furniture. To the rear are a host of attractions including café, farm shop and Cannon Hall Farm, a great attraction for families.

The onward route runs along the house front and past a walled garden into shrubbery. Remain on the main path which swings down to the right, soon reaching a stone archway. To your right is Fairyland, where a small pool sits amid modest stone follies. Through the arch you cross a footbridge back into open parkland, and a good path drops down the hedgeside to rejoin the outward route at the bottom corner. Return over the bridge to retrace steps as far as Dark Lane, and this time go straight ahead through trees the short way to a setted ford and clapper bridge on Tanyard Beck, a nice corner. Across, take the broad, hollowed Cliff Hill Lane rising right, winding up to re-enter the village centre opposite Maltkiln Row. Go left to finish.

Opposite: Cawthorne church   *Cannon Hall*

2³4 miles from Surprise View

Easy moorland paths in Yorkshire's corner of the Peak District

Start *National Park car park (SK 252801; S11 7TZ) on A6187 2 miles south of Hathersage*
Map *OS Explorer OL1, Peak District, Dark Peak*

From the car park's eastern end, a path heads away between fence and road. Within a couple of minutes take a small gate in the fence, and ignoring a path heading away, turn right on a path parallel with the fence. This runs along the moor edge, through silver birch into more open terrain. At a fork keep right near the fence, running grandly on to reach a stream crossing. Resuming, you soon reach a gate sending a footpath through the fence. Of two paths heading away onto the moor, take the second one rising gently alongside a bouldery knoll on your right. At an early fork on the brow keep left up this gentle spur: ahead to your right is flat-topped Carl Wark, with the bolder frame of Higger Tor beyond. Shortly after a fork from which both branches soon re-unite, the path drops right off the spur to run through bracken to a junction on the edge of reeds. Turn left on this grand path rising gently in the well-defined boundary between bracken and reeds. Levelling out on a sombre plateau, keep right at a fork to cross to the foot of the firmer slopes of Carl Wark. The path makes a brief climb to a path junction on its westerly shoulder. Turn right, rising very steadily the short way to an old information panel just short of the brow.

Carl Wark appears a classic example of an Iron Age hillfort dating back perhaps 2500 years, but experts suggest a 5th or 6th century relic of the Dark Ages. Both may be right, with an older fort re-established after the Romans departed, by British tribes as defence against Anglian invaders. This natural site is defended on three sides by steep scarps of gritstone boulders, with a wide turf rampart supporting the mighty wall at this open western end. That wall stands just yards above you to the left. Either take the left path to it, or the path straight up onto the plateau to enjoy views across to Burbage Rocks from the craggy eastern edge.

Leave by returning to the wall, where the main path drops briefly right onto flatter terrain. The onward path heads for Higger Tor, but just 20 yards beyond a near-immediate cross-paths, take an inviting grassy branch curving left into bracken. Rising slightly, it undulates through bracken, heather and moor-grass to merge with a path dropping from Higger Tor. Keep on, ignoring a left branch and advance to the corner of a walled enclosure. Pass along its right side to a path junction at the far corner. Turn left here on a broad path that quickly diverges from the wall, rising gently right onto a heathery brow with Over Owler Tor ahead. It runs over a lesser cross-path in the little defile of Winyards Nick and along to the waiting boss of rock that is Over Owler Tor.

A brief rise through boulders leads to its broad top, a fine vantage point with the end of the walk only ten minutes away. Excellent views look westward across the Derwent Valley into the heart of the Peak District. Resume on the path curving down to gain the isolated tor of Mother Cap just below you. From here resume gently downhill to a scattering of boulders and into some colourful silver birch to reveal the car park just two minutes ahead. A kissing-gate puts you back into it.

Opposite: Boulders on Carl Wark   *Mother Cap*

Index • *walk number refers*

Flamborough

Hebden Bridge

Muker